CHILDREN

of

Catastrophe

CHILDREN
of
Catastrophe

Journey from a
Palestinian Refugee
Camp to America

JAMAL KRAYEM KANJ

Garnet
PUBLISHING

CHILDREN OF CATASTROPHE
Journey from a Palestinian Refugee Camp to America

Published by
Garnet Publishing Limited
8 Southern Court
South Street
Reading
RG1 4QS
UK

www.garnetpublishing.co.uk

First Edition

ISBN-13: 978-1-85964-262-7

British Library Cataloguing-in-Publication Data
A catalogue record for this book is available from the British Library

Typeset by Samantha Barden
Jacket design by David Rose
Cover photos used courtesy of UNRWA/J. Madvo
and Jamal Krayem Kanj

Printed and bound in Lebanon by International Press:
interpress@int-press.com

To Krayem,
Noora & Nahr el Bared Camp

Contents

— —

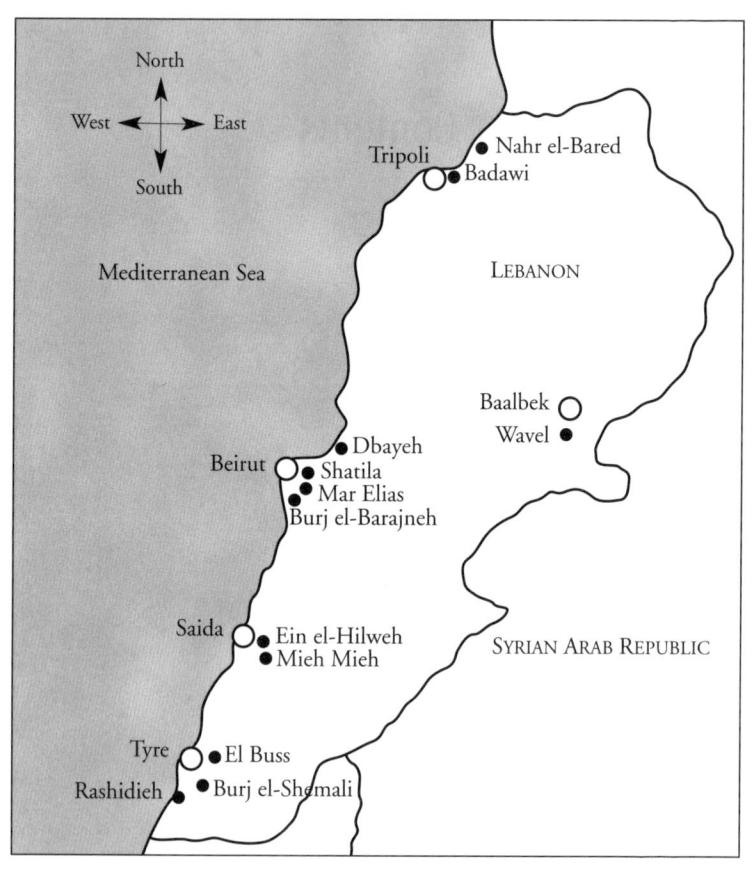

● PALESTINIAN REFUGEE CAMPS IN LEBANON

Preface

--

There are many individuals that I would like to acknowledge for making this book a reality: some who have directly encouraged me to write, and others who supported me consciously or unconsciously by listening to the stories shared in this book.

At first, I hesitated to take the book project very seriously but for two major motivations: first, my children, with whom I shared some of the book's accounts as they blossomed at a young age; and second, my parents, without whom there would have been no story to tell. For the children, I wanted to connect them with their roots far from their comfortable home in California, and for my parents, a deserving tribute to preserve their memory beyond life.

I knew writing a book was going to be a long and protracted project. I remember reading George Orwell's 1953 book, *England Your England*, where he aptly etched: "Writing a book is a horrible, exhausting struggle, like a long bout of some painful illness." As Orwell did, I understood the challenge, especially since the text had political and historical nuances and not just a personal narrative.

Finally an opportunity materialized when I left San Diego for a job on the island of Bahrain. With very few friends on the island, I had much free time after work and during weekends. To fill the time, I started in late 2006 to find a quiet corner at home or at the Seef, and later in the city center's Caribou Coffee, to sketch down the story. I told myself that even if nothing came out of it, at least it would be a written legacy for my children.

At times, like Orwell, it was indeed an "exhausting struggle" recording my internal emotions onto a lifeless computer. Nevertheless, soon after I began to organize my thoughts, jog down the general ideas and review my writings, I started to enjoy the project. For the first time, I was able to see the story from afar, not just as the person who lived the events but also as part of an audience. I discovered another by-product of the writing, a soothing therapeutic experience while searching for the soul of humanity in all the events and the people I got to know and grew up with in the camp. At the end, Orwell must have failed to mention that completing a book could also signal the start of a lifetime healing process.

I planned and canceled two visits to the camp in the summer of 2006 and 2007. The first was due to Israel's 33-day war against Lebanon and the second a full-blown battle between Fatah al Islam and the Lebanese army. The 2007 confrontations culminated in the complete destruction of the camp. This event is detailed in Chapter 9.

The events of 2007 added new emphasis to the story of a camp that had progressed from a place of destitution in 1949 to a lively self-sufficient community in 2007. With its destruction, the shared stories in the book took on new meanings and created an additional urgency to record the collective memory of this faded place. Indeed, the stories in this book are owned equally by the people who were left homeless again sixty years following their first expulsion from Palestine. Since I was in a position to do so, I felt it was my obligation to share their fate with the rest of the world.

I stayed in touch with my parents by phone following the clashes of summer 2007. We talked almost every Thursday, but I failed to make a call on the last Thursday of January 2008. Then, on the following Sunday evening, 3 February, we received a frantic call from my sister Aziza in San Diego with the news that my mother had suffered a serious stroke.

I came to learn afterwards that, on the prior Friday, my dad had received special military clearance to visit the remnants of their home in the destroyed camp. Up until then, my mother had harbored some hopes that the house or their lifelong possessions might still be recovered. In the evening, my father came back to tell her "*Al'awad Bi Allah*", "Our ultimate compensation is with God." In other words, everything was gone.

Next morning, while talking with my sister on the phone, my mother became incoherent and out of nowhere began telling Aziza that "Jamal" would be calling today. The following day she suffered a debilitating stroke. Even though my mother survived, she has not convalesced fully, eventually losing her sight and much of her short-term memory. Following the second dispossession of their lifetime, my father's new purpose is now to comfort her throughout her grave disability. Although she ended up losing her vision, my mother never lost her foresight. Her insight shall remain a guiding light in the darkest alleys of my life.

Recognizing my powerlessness to help my parents persevere much longer, I hope by sharing their lifelong struggle or "jihad", their memories and that of the Palestinian refugees in Nahr el Bared will live throughout the pages of this book in perpetuity.

Most of the people who provided invaluable advice throughout the writing process shall remain nameless. However, I would particularly like to acknowledge friends such as Ed and Ethel Sweed, who reviewed and critiqued the first of the many drafts, the counsel and encouragement I received from long-time friends Jim Rauch and Doris Bittar, and the support I received from those individuals with whom I share a common struggle and commitment to human justice, such as Yousef Abu Dayyeh, Larry Christian, Basheer Idoui, Stephanie Jennings, the late Terry Christian, and the many others who knowingly or unknowingly influenced my writing. Special thanks are due to Garnet Publishing, especially to the commissioning editor Dan Nunn who made this possible.

A deep heartfelt appreciation goes to my five brothers Ghazi, Majed, Kamal, Kamel, Abed el Nasser and my sister Aziza, who collectively inspired me to reach for the maximum potentials in my journey to a new American home.

My gratitude would be incomplete without expressing my deepest appreciation to Taghrid, the woman with whom I share two loving sons, Naseem al Carmel and Bassel Jamal, and an adorable daughter, Kenana Noora: for you are the utmost reasons I strive to excel in life.

Lastly but not least, this book is dedicated to my father Krayem for challenging my human limitations, and for my mother Noora whose bottomless compassion made me a better human being, and finally to Nahr el Bared Refugee Camp, home to the *Children of Catastrophe*.

Introduction

— —

This book is about growing up in a Palestinian refugee camp in Lebanon, and about the refugees' intractable resolve to survive and succeed.

While all refugees suffered the same terrible problem of adjusting from statehood to statelessness, the refugees in Lebanon represented a special and unique case. From the outset, Palestinian refugees in Lebanon were treated as foreigners with no social, labour or political rights. Unlike refugees in the West Bank and Jordan who were granted citizenship, and Syria where refugees were accorded full residency privileges, Palestinian refugees in Lebanon were prohibited from working in more than seventy trades and professions. The Lebanese government instituted special regulations restricting the movement of refugees within the state and limited their ability to build or to own property in the country.

BACKGROUND
The creation of the State of Israel in 1948 culminated in the

displacement of 805,067 Palestinians and the destruction of 531 indigenous villages, resulting in the expulsion of roughly 85 per cent of the native population and the seizure of 92 per cent of the land.

Meanwhile, Britain, the recognized mandate power, abdicated its moral responsibility towards the colonized native population when, under its tutelage, it facilitated the arming, empowering and the resettlement of foreign Europeans in Palestine. In fact, more than fifty per cent (413,790) of the Palestinian refugees were forced out of their homes by the Zionists while Palestine was still ostensibly a British protectorate.[1]

The expulsion of the native population by the Zionists was part of a systematic and deliberate programme which began at the turn of the nineteenth century. In response to the rise of European anti-Semitism, Theodore Herzl, the Hungarian founder of modern political Zionism, advocated a Jewish homeland in whatever land "is given to us".[2] To arrogate the "real estate" deal with illegitimate colonial land brokers, the Zionist leadership exhibited portentous apathy toward the indigenous population. For the Zionists, the natives were either expendable transferable objects or a disregarded nuisance.

In 1896 Herzl described the ominous plan in his diary:

> We shall endeavor to expel the poor population across the border unnoticed, procuring employment for it in transit countries, but denying it any employment in our own country.[3]

The Zionist leadership contemplated places such as Argentina, Cyprus, Sinai and Uganda as potential locations for their proposed homeland. Regarding Argentina, in his book *Der Judenstaat*, or *The Jewish State*, Herzl wrote:

> Argentina is one of the most fertile countries in the world … The
> Argentine Republic would derive considerable profit from the
> cession of a portion of its territory to us.

With regard to Palestine as another option, and attempting
to exploit the Ottoman Empire's dire financial straits, Herzl
wrote in the subsequent paragraph:

> If his Majesty the Sultan were to give us Palestine, we could in
> return undertake to regulate the whole finances of Turkey.

When the financially troubled sick man of Europe (Turkey)
rejected the generous funding offer, and as other alternatives
became less attainable, the Zionists turned their eyes toward
the likely World War I victor and the new colonizer in the
region, Great Britain.

To that end, Zionist lobbying succeeded in 1917 to
bring about the British government's letter to a wealthy
Jewish banker, Baron Rothschild, in what otherwise became
known as the Balfour Declaration. The letter promised the
banker the British government's intent was to help establish "a
national home for the Jewish people" in Palestine. Following
World War I, Great Britain, the new victors' self-designated
mandate authority, appointed a professed British Zionist,
Sir Herbert Samuel, as the High Commissioner for Palestine.
In his role, Samuel facilitated new European immigration to
the territory to help transform the demographics of the local
population with the new Jewish settlers.

Nearly fifty years following Herzl's 1896 prophecy, the
Zionist's "Transfer Committee", headed by the first Israeli
prime minister, Ben Gurion, consciously or unconsciously
assigned jargon tantamount to ethnic cleansing to their
military operations, from names such as *matateh* (broom),
tihur (cleansing), *biur* (a Passover expression meaning "to

cleanse the leaven") and *niku* (a Hebrew word for cleaning up).[4]

This was a plan which Joseph Weitz, the head of the National Jewish Fund, described in his diary on 20 December 1940 as:

> Not one village must be left, not one [Bedouin] tribe. The transfer must be directed at Iraq, Syria, and even Transjordan.[5]

NAHR EL BARED CAMP

Palestinian refugees who settled in Lebanon came mostly from towns and villages in the northern part of historical Palestine. Naturally at first, most of the refugees settled in southern Lebanon, in proximity to their homes across the border. However, to avoid potential conflicts with Israel, the Lebanese authorities decided to relocate the refugees from the southern borders and divide them into smaller groups. As an adjunct to this, several UN humanitarian services were created to help the newly established refugee camps throughout Lebanon.* The UN emergency aid services to the temporary refugee camps were led at first by a network of the League of Red Cross Societies, the American Friends Service Committee, Non-governmental Organizations (NGOs) and other UN organizations.

In November 1948, the UN established the United Nations Relief for Palestinian Refugees (UNRPR) as an umbrella organization to coordinate the work efforts of the NGOs and other UN agencies. On 8 December 1949,

---

* Four of the camps were eventually destroyed and removed either by Israeli invasions or as a result of the Lebanese Civil War. Today twelve Palestinian refugee camps remain in Lebanon.

the UN General Assembly voted for the establishment of the United Nations Relief and Works Agency (UNRWA). UNRWA started its operations in May 1950, with a renewable mandate every three years, to provide services to all registered Palestinian refugees.

The replacement of the interim relief agencies with UNRWA was intended to provide long-term relief and work for Palestinian refugees. However, leaders of the Palestinian refugee community were concerned that the new organization was part of a larger international covert program emphasizing long-term settlement, and de-emphasizing the need to implement UN resolution 194 calling for the refugees' right of return to their original homes.

Nahr el Bared Camp was initially founded by the League of Red Cross Societies (LRCS) in 1949 to service refugees relocated from the south and from the region of the Beqaa Valley (A'njar) in eastern Lebanon. The camp was situated on the Mediterranean shorelines, approximately ten miles north of the city of Tripoli and about fifteen miles from the Syrian borders. It was built on the shore of Nahr el Bared, which means "Cold River" in English, hence the name Nahr el Bared Camp, along the main highway linking Lebanon with Syria and far from any major Lebanese population centres.

The main road became an important economic lifeline for trading and commercial activities servicing the surrounding Lebanese towns and villages, as further explained in Chapter 5 of this book, on the camp's economy. Likewise, the river and the sea equally played very important roles in sustaining its future economy. Early on, the river was the only available semi-clean source of running water for refugees to bathe and to wash their clothing in. The sea was an important source of fishing, construction aggregates and trade.

TRANSFORMATIONS

The camp experienced approximately five major transformations following its establishment in 1949. In the early years, it was a muddy clump of tents over an area of less than one square mile for a population of fewer than 5,000 inhabitants. In the mid- to late 1950s residents started to replace the temporary tents with permanent huts; in the early 1970s, having a soaring population of about 18,000, the camp went through a construction boom to accommodate this increase. In 1982, a new wave of refugees escaping the Israeli invasion and occupation of southern Lebanon took shelter in the camp. In the late 1980s and early 1990s the camp started to expand outside its official boundaries into what later became known as the new camp. In the summer of 2007, the camp was completely destroyed by the Lebanese army.

Despite the population's natal growth between 1949 and 1969, the area of the camp remained unchanged as people were not permitted to expand beyond the original demarcation lines established by the Red Cross in 1949. Furthermore, the Lebanese authorities imposed severe limits on building permits, even for minor expansions or simple home renovations inside the camp proper. In the early years, residents were not even permitted to build restrooms inside their properties and had to use public latrines built by UNRWA. Camp inhabitants were not permitted to build concrete roofs or to pave infront of their courtyards. Water was to be carried physically from community public fountains and the digging of water wells was strictly controlled.

There were also harsh security and civil measures taken against persons suspected of political activities. I knew of individuals who were relocated by the Lebanese Interior Security from refugee camps in the south for being suspected of, or arrested for, trying to cross the borders illicitly to visit their homes and properties under Israeli occupation. These individuals were placed under partial house arrest and were required to show up twice a day at the hated Interior Security Office to prove their continued presence in the camp.

Following the camp uprising in 1969, which resulted in the withdrawal of the Lebanese security forces and the entry of the Palestine Liberation Organization (PLO), the camp experienced significant construction activities to ease overcrowding and to meet natural population growth. Initially the new construction was mostly to replace dilapidated tin roofs, carry out overdue renovations and room expansions within homes. Later, as a result of demand and the lack of any official building authority oversight, home dwellers encroached onto public alleyways and open space areas throughout the camp. Thirty years later, the camp had become one of the most densely overcrowded square miles in the world.

In 1982 and following the Israeli invasion and the displacement of refugees from southern Lebanon, the PLO acquired a small piece of land adjacent to the northern boundary of the camp to house the new group of refugees. Since Palestinians cannot legally purchase or own property in Lebanon, the PLO had to deed the land to the Lebanese Islamic endowment. Subsequently, Lebanese land owners in the adjoining properties began to subdivide their land and offered it for sale to interested buyers. Several residents invested their life savings in purchasing new plots of land, which frequently remained under the name of the Lebanese land owner but with a real estate "power of attorney" in the purchaser's name. The new area became known as the new camp. I shall elaborate further in the coming chapters on the development of the camp from penurious conditions to becoming a major commercial hub competing with traders in the second largest city in Lebanon, and then to the eventual destruction of the camp.

THE FUTURE

Since 1948, and having professed otherwise at first, Israel has consistently blocked the implementation of UN resolution 194* ordering the return of refugees to their original homes. It used diplomacy as a tactic to prolong negotiations indefinitely‡ (negotiation for the sake of negotiation) while it continued to transform the demographics on the ground, preempting the outcome of future peace talks. It continues to do so today by building illegal settlements in the area slated for negotiation between Israel and the Palestinian Authority. No doubt Israel has mastered the art of temporizing in its diplomacy: as a past president of the World Jewish Organization, Nahum Goldman once said, in the mid-1970s, that "Diplomacy in the Middle East is the art of delaying the inevitable as long as possible."[6] The passage of time, however, has so far failed to change the resolve of the refugees. Instead of taking responsibility for driving the Palestinians from their homes, Israel deludes itself into hoping that time will metamorphose the refugees into a mirage in the vast Arabian landscape. In analyzing Palestinian refugee concerns after 1948, an Israeli Foreign Ministry official document projected that:

> The most adaptable and best survivors would 'manage' by a process of natural selection and others will waste away. Some will die but most will turn into human debris and social outcasts and probably join the poorest classes in the Arab countries. [State Archives, FM, 2444/19][7]

---

* Israel also continues to evade compliance with UN Security Council's Resolutions 242, 338 and the US road map.

‡ Following the Madrid negotiations sponsored by the first Bush administration, Israeli prime minister, Yitzhak Shamir, admitted his strategy was to deliberately drag negotiations on for a decade.

To the chagrin of Israeli protagonists, the refugees' identity became an expression of nationhood and defiance, rather than privation and compliance. Today, the mere survival of the Palestinian refugees continues to prove the fallacy of the Israeli prophecy more than sixty years earlier. Instead, the refugees have indefatigably remained part of a nation, without the state. Israeli writer Danny Rubinstein said it best when describing the Palestinians in his book:

> Every people in the world lives in a place. For Palestinians, the place lives in them.[8]

Notes

1   See the Palestine Land Society map at www.plands.org/map_english.htm, retrieved May 2008.
2   Isseroff, Ami, 'The history of Zionism and the creation of Israel', http://www.mideastweb.org/zionism.htm, retrieved June 2009.
3   Pappé, Ilan, *The Ethnic Cleansing of Palestine* (Oxford: Oneworld Publications, 2006), p. 250.
4   Ibid.
5   Masallah, Nur, *Expulsion of the Palestinians: The Concept of Transfer in Zionist Political Thought* (Washington, DC: Institute for Palestine Studies, 1992), pp. 131–32.
6   Safiah, Afif, 'Diplomacy in the Middle East: The Art of Delaying the Inevitable', July 2001, http://www.passia.org/publications/Pal-Id/afif06.pdf, retrieved 4 December 2008.
7   Segev, Tom, and Weinstein, Arlen Neal, *1949 The First Israelis* (New York: Owl Books by Henry Holt and Company, 1998), p. 30. (Quoted originally from: Middle East Information, 'The Problem of Arab Refugees', State Archive, Foreign Ministry, Refugees, 2444/19.)
8   Rubinstein, Danny, *The People of Nowhere: The Palestinian Vision of Homeland* (New York: Times Books, 1991), p. 120.

1

The Making of a Refugee

—-

"You can take the boy out of the country, but you can't take the country out of the boy." This is a Rwandan proverb I first heard in the early 1980s while watching a *60 Minutes* interview with American actor and singer Dean Reed who was self-exiled in the former East Germany. Reed was talking about his deep connections to his home in America. I was also taken from my home, but before birth. I was born ten years after my parents were expelled from their homes in Palestine. Yet Palestine must have been embedded in my DNA structure. In this case the proverb could fittingly be restated, "You can take the egg out of the country, but you can't take the country out of the egg."

I come originally from an old Palestinian Arab tribe known as "Arab Al Haib". The equivalent English translation of Al Haib is "those with 'charismatic demeanour'". My family belonged to the tribal branch that settled the shores of Palestine north of Acre and next to a town called Al Zeeb. My parents were married around 1940 when my father was about sixteen years old and my mother had barely reached puberty. She tells the story that while playing in the neighbourhood with friends of her age, she was told, "You are marrying Krayem". The story goes that Krayem's father Nayef settled a debt with Noora's father Ghathian, who in turn agreed to wed Noora to Krayem. The young teenagers Noora and Krayem did not have any choice but to honour the arrangement made between their elders. Since they married so young, seven years passed before the birth of their first child in 1947. Ghazi, my oldest brother, was born several years after Palestine became a preferred refuge destination for Jews escaping the early Nazi repression and later the Nazi Holocaust in Europe. My father told me years later that Palestinians at first welcomed the new immigrant European Jews as there was already a small native Jewish community living peacefully in Palestine. However, by the 1930s it became clear to the indigenous population that the new wave of European immigrants, abetted by the British occupiers, was part of a much larger Zionist plan to replace the native Palestinians and establish a Jewish homeland instead.

Palestinian Jews were for the most part successful artisans, especially in carpentry, and lived around the city of Jerusalem. Native Jews were skilled merchants who passed down their trades within the family from generation to generation. Besides, members of the native Jewish community, as well as their fellow upper-class native Palestinians, exhibited little interest in agriculture and considered farming an inferior trade, and farmers as a primitive class of people.

However, and unlike the native Jewish community, the new European immigrants established exclusive Jewish settlements far from Jerusalem, showed special interest in land acquisition and less interest in the archetypal native Jewish pious tradition around the holy city of Jerusalem. The aggressive land ownership activities and the exclusionary farming communities established by the new immigrants, segregated even from the native Jewish community, roused the suspicion of native Palestinians. Little did the Palestinians know at the time about the forty-year-old furtive program of the Zionist Jewish National Fund (JNF) to purchase land to benefit and encourage European Jewish immigration to Palestine ...

The JNF was established by the Fifth Zionist Congress in 1901 to purchase land and to lease it "exclusively to Jews at a nominal rate".[1] JNF strategy promoted the Zionist's slogan, "conquest of labour" (*Kibbush avodah*), which advocated the hiring of "Jews and only Jews"[2] while denying "employment" to the "poor population" as envisaged by the founder of Zionism, Theodore Herzl, several years earlier.

Nearly fifty years later, by the time of the creation of the state of Israel, the JNF and the Zionist movement had only managed to acquire about 7 per cent of the land of Palestine, or 1,585,365 dunums.[3] In his book *The Birth of the Palestinian Refugee Problem*, Israeli author Benny Morris confirms that by 1947, Jewish land ownership in Palestine was less than 7 per cent.[4] This fact was corroborated, to a degree, by the Jewish National Fund, which stated that "By the time Israel declared independence in 1948, the JNF owned 12.5 per cent of all the land of Israel."[5]

Since 1948, the JNF has led an international scheme to cover up the destroyed Palestinian villages with a specious environmental forestation campaign promoting the planting of trees in Israel.

The JNF boasts that it "... has planted over 240 million trees in the land of Israel".[6] The JNF does not, however, disclose to its unsuspected donors that at least eighty-six of these forests and parks are built over the ruins of destroyed Palestinian villages.[7] I visited some of the sites disguised as parks and forests to see old chiseled stones from demolished homes and mulish cactus plants sprouting, which exposed Israel and the JNF's gambit to hide the evidence of emptied and destroyed villages. As an example, the well-known Israeli Canada Park was built on the ruins of the ethnically cleansed villages of Emmuas, Yalu and Bayt Nuba; the trees in Biriya Forest grow over the foundation of the village of Amuka; the town of Reihaniyeh is buried under Ramat Menashe Park and the remains of Ajur are fertilizing the greenery in Park Britain.[8]

Where the JNF did not reforest what were once peaceful villages and as part of Israel's conjured history, Israel has bestowed Hebrew pseudonyms on the locations, replacing the native names of Palestinian towns. Thus, Tel Rabi became Tel Aviv, Lubya turned into Lavi, Al Zeeb transpired into Gesher Haziv, Saffuriyya into Tzippori and Beit Jala metamorphosed into Gilo.

JOURNEY INTO REFUGEE LIFE

Ignoring the facts on the ground, on 29 November 1947 and under pressure from the British and cohorts of guilt-ridden Western governments, the United Nations General Assembly voted to partition Palestine between the native Palestinians and the new Jewish immigrants. Under the UN plan, the native Palestinians who owned 93 per cent of Palestine were offered less than 44 per cent of their registered properties, while the Zionist movement, who held less than 7 per cent, was awarded more than 56 per cent of the land. Naturally, the Palestinians rejected the UN plan as unjust and called for a fair resolution that recognized the rights of the indigenous landowners.

The proposed partition of Palestine was part of the United Nations Special Committee's (UNSCOP) recommendation to divide the country into three parts, a Palestinian state with a population of 735,000, of which 725,000 were Palestinians and 10,000 Jews; a new Jewish state comprised of 499,000 Jews and 407,000 Palestinians, with roughly less than a 60 per cent Jewish majority. The internationally governed third part of the UNSCOP proposal was to be the holy city of Jerusalem, the population of which was to be equally divided between Jews and Palestinians.[9]

While publicly professing to accept the UN proposal, the Zionist leadership was unhappy with the partition plan. The Zionists, who were to be given what wasn't theirs in the first place, were surreptitiously disappointed by the large proportional number of native Palestinians in the newly allocated Jewish state. In addressing the Central Committee of the Histadrut (the Eretz Israel Workers Party) several days after the UN vote to partition Palestine, Ben-Gurion expressed his apprehension about the UN plan when he stated:

> … the total population of the Jewish State at the time of its establishment will be about one million, including almost 40% non-Jews. Such a [population] composition does not provide a stable basis for a Jewish state. This [demographic] fact must be viewed in all its clarity and acuteness. With such a [population] composition, there cannot even be absolute certainty that control will remain in the hands of the Jewish majority … There can be no stable and strong Jewish state so long as it has a Jewish majority of only 60%.[10]

To ensure with "absolute certainty" a Jewish exclusivity, the Zionist paramilitary organizations began to wage a meticulous and coordinated military campaign to "cleanse" historical

Palestine of its non-Jewish population (Operations Gimmel, Delet, Hiram, Scissors, Broom, Cleaning up, Yaov ... etc.)[11]

The expulsion of my parents from their home was the beginning of a long-lasting journey into the life of a refugee. While my parents were always fond of talking about their memories of Palestine, they rarely mentioned the details of their expulsion from their homes. At last, I asked my mother and father separately to tell me about that experience in 1948. Soon after the massacre of Palestinian civilians in Deir Yassin on 9 April 1948, at the hands of the Zionist Irgun and Lehi terrorist organizations, my father joined the Arab Liberation Army (ALA). He left his wife and baby with his elderly parents to join the fight for the future of Palestine. Established by the Arab League in 1947, the ALA was comprised of non-regular volunteers and was led by an ex-army officer from Syria.

Meanwhile my mother and her in-laws were forced to leave their homes ahead of the advancing Zionist paramilitaries from the coastal town of Al Zeeb, and moved inland toward a village called Al Kabri. They mistakenly thought the departure from their homes was a short jaunt to just another nearby Palestinian town, but as the Zionist military pressure continued, they were compelled again to move from Al Kabri to other villages in northern Palestine. My mother stated that the family continued to move from one town to another ahead of the advancing Jewish terrorists as they assaulted and murdered civilians in the nearby villages of Al Tantora, Sofsaf and Sa'ssa between February and October of 1948. Subsequent to my mother's testimony, I conducted a search and discovered detailed personal accounts of these and other massacres.[12]

Back in his new irregular army unit, my father was disappointed by the ALA's poor organization and its lack of military readiness. Other than lip service, the newly independent yet vassal Arab governments offered no real help to the irregular Arab volunteers or the Palestinians at large. My father confided to me that their unit was ordered on 15 May 1948 to defend only the Palestinian designated areas under the UN partition plan and to refrain from any attack against the Jewish parts. Following Israel's unilateral declaration of independence, to satisfy its insatiable expansionist land-grab strategy and to secure an "absolute Jewish majority", the Zionists assailed, depopulated and occupied an additional 30 per cent of the land which had been designated for the future Palestinian state under the UN plan. The ALA was outnumbered and outmanoeuvred by the British-supplied and trained Jewish Haganah. In an ensuing ceasefire, the ALA was forced to abandon its positions and was withdrawn to Syria.

At that point, no one knew the whereabouts of my father, whether he was dead or alive. In late 1948 and with a baby in her arms, my mother joined her in-laws and thousands of other Palestinians fleeing ahead of advancing Zionist militants to seek refuge in Lebanon. They stopped for a short time in south Lebanon and soon were relocated to the eastern part, before finally settling north in a new refugee camp next to Nahr el Bared, or "Cold River" in English. The camp came to be known later as Nahr el Bared Camp.

My father had no means of contacting his family. He didn't know whether they were dead or alive either; whether they remained under occupation or had been relocated to one of the newly established refugee camps. A short time after arriving in an area called A'njar in eastern Lebanon, my grandmother beseeched her son-in-law to try to find out what had happened to her son. Abu Salah went looking for my father at several known ALA military centres and, after a long search, he found him in a military base in Damascus,

Syria. Soon thereafter, the ALA was dismantled and my father was reunited with his family in A'njar before relocating to north Lebanon.

In the meantime, the new refugee life and the creation of the state of Israel meant that my grandfather was forever separated from his only sister, Amsha. Amsha and her brother were separated in the midst of the Jewish military thrust into the Galilee area in late May 1948. Amid fear and confusion, Amsha, along with her three young daughters, lost contact with her brother and took refuge in another Palestinian town that soon fell under the control of Jewish military groups and remained in what later became the State of Israel.

As a young child I heard my father talking about his aunt and her three daughters who evaded expulsion and remained behind in their homeland. He talked about how his father had died without being able to see his only sister. With tear-filled eyes he told me that not only had my grandfather never been able to see his sister again, but even after he died they were not able to inform her that her only brother had passed away. The same story was repeated again in the late 1960s when Amsha herself died. Although she was his only aunt, my father didn't learn of her death until several years later. My mother would usually interject by saying, "I wish we'd stayed behind too, for I would have rather lived under cruel occupation on my land and not in the heavens of someone else's land." By losing their country, my grandfather and his sister died as strangers, one in her homeland that was no more, and the other as a refugee without a home.

Almost fifty years later and under unusual circumstances, I met with Amsha's three daughters when, in 1996, they visited me at the Hadassah Hospital's emergency room in Jerusalem, an encounter I will discuss later in this book.

A MOTHER'S CURSE

The ethnic cleansing of the native Palestinians was a human catastrophe of enormous proportion. Many of the tragedies went unrecorded and untold, or were even silenced. I came to know of a moving story about a relative named Abu Musa. In 1948, ahead of advancing Zionist terrorists, Abu Musa evacuated his family, including his wife, a newborn baby and his blind and physically disabled mother. During their disorganised flight, they were spotted and attacked by the Jewish Haganah air force. Abu Musa panicked and dropped his disabled mother in a ditch on the side of the road and continued to run for shelter with his wife and baby.

As the Jewish military continued to shell the roads and nearby Palestinian villages, Abu Musa was unable to go back to check on his mother until the next day. During a lull in the air raids, Abu Musa went back to the spot where he had left his mother. She was nowhere to be found. He looked around and ran into local villagers who had come back to check on their properties. He asked the men if they had seen a disabled woman around the road. They told him that they had just buried the remains of what had appeared to be the body of a woman torn apart by wild animals.

After finding out that his mother had been violently killed by wild animals, Abu Musa was hysterical and blamed himself for leaving his helpless mother on the side of the road. He spent days and nights talking to people about what might have happened to his mother. He was desperately seeking answers to alleviate his anguish; had saving his infant baby been worth it? Had his mother indeed been eaten alive? Or had she been killed by the air raid? He was traumatized and his life was never the same again. The loss of his home and his mother were just the start of a long life of grief for Abu Musa.

Abu Musa ended up settling in the same camp as my parents. In addition to his first baby, he had three more children in the camp, two boys and a girl. He lived a tragic and lugubrious life until he died in the mid 1990s. Everyone who knew him believed that he must have lived with his mother's curse. In the early 1970s, his eldest son, Musa, tried to sneak back into the approximate area where his grandmother had died. He was spotted by Israeli soldiers and killed instantly. Israel did not repatriate Musa's body to his family. Abu Musa, who had never seen his mother's dead body, was unable to see or bury his eldest son either. His only consolation was that Musa had died in the same area where the remains of his grandmother had been buried about twenty-four years earlier. Musa had left Palestine as an infant, but like salmon intuitively swimming back to their birthplace against all the odds, he had gone back to die there as an adult.

A short time after he lost his first son, Abu Musa became disabled. I made it a point to call on him whenever I visited the camp. It broke my heart when, during my last stopover, I saw Abu Musa coming out of the bathroom crawling like a little baby. I kneeled down to kiss him; he kissed me back, and then asked, "Who are you, my son?"

Misery was not alien to Abu Musa and his family. In the early 1990s he also lost his youngest son, Kamal. Kamal was going to school in Tripoli when a local militia at a checkpoint ordered him out of his taxi. He was literally butchered. Kamal was murdered the year he was to have graduated from high school.

Until his death, Abu Musa's only wish was to die and be buried close to his mother and eldest son. But even a death wish is too much for a Palestinian refugee to be able to realize. He lived for almost fifty years following his expulsion from Palestine. After the loss of his mother, he ended up having two of his three sons killed and was disabled for more than twenty-five years. Abu Musa's life was the heartbreaking tale of just another Palestinian refugee. Was it his mother's curse that had followed him for all those years?

DEPRIVATION BY CIRCUMSTANCE

Children are born within a predetermined environment of fortune or hardship. Other than the first common breath of fresh air, newborns are ordained to become part of the collective circumstance of their social surroundings. It is predestined by default from before birth that we are either privileged or deprived by circumstance.

Life in the camp was deprivation by circumstance. The circumstance for the most part had been created to advance privileges to other humans. From time immemorial, human privileges have been advanced by war and colonial expansion, and recently by the exploitation of human and natural resources via economic means and political domination. Advancing human privileges by conquest and colonial expansion resulted in devastation and deprivation to many of the aboriginal people.

The ethnic cleansing of Palestine, however, was not driven purely by the simple need to conquer another people, or for economic greed. The conquest, political domination and economic exploitation were merely by-products of a goal that intended to solve the dispossession of Jews in Christian Europe. The objectives in the conquest of Palestine were to provide a safe haven for the victims of the European Nazi Holocaust. The European Zionist movement, supported by a guilt-ridden West, wanted to provide safe harbour for European Jews while at the same time subjugating the land of Palestine, but in this case without its native people. Almost for the first time in history, a deprived class of people was privileged by depriving another group of humans of the same; thus, the creation of the Palestine refugee problem.

Like other Palestinian refugees, when my parents first left their homes in Palestine, they took with them only the basic essentials for what they thought would be a short period away from home. However, the temporary evacuation became a voyage of no return after which the indigent Palestinians had to settle in new refugee camps in neighbouring countries. The new refugees had to start building their lives from scratch. At first they survived on the scraps provided by a newly created UN organization, the United Nations Relief and Works Agency for Palestinian Refugees (UNRWA).

UNRWA was established by the United Nations General Assembly Resolution 302 (IV) on 8 December 1949, to help settle and create jobs for Palestinian refugees. Finding jobs to survive was the next challenge for the people in the camp. In addition to work as labourers on the neighbouring Lebanese farms and in construction, the UN agency became the largest employer of Palestinian refugees. UNRWA established sanitation crews to collect refuse, and recruited teachers, janitors, medical assistants, etc. My father landed a job first as a sanitation labourer, before becoming, years later, an ambulance driver serving the two UN camps in north Lebanon.

THE NEW COMMUNITY

The camp's population make-up was atypical of any conventional township formation. Communities in the Middle East usually go through lengthy historical processes before developing into villages, towns or cities. It takes communities hundreds of years before becoming fully fledged and diverse societies. The family history and hierarchy is often the embryo for the emergence of villages and townships. Inter-marriages between neighbouring populations transform the single family structure into large extended families. Labour and services exchange between localities weakens the family dominance, hence a natural progression towards fully matured communities, villages and towns.

The development of the camp, however, skipped all the normal historical evolution of townships. Members of the new community came from all sorts of backgrounds and localities. Landowners, farmers, city dwellers, Bedouins, doyens, family chiefs (*mukhtars*), professionals, rich and poor all found themselves living and sharing a new communal life. A nomadic Bedouin was living next to a city dweller, a landowner was residing next to a farm labourer and *mukhtars* competed for power and authority. Local neighbourhoods immediately became prototypes of old villages as the camp was informally divided by refugees based on the origin of their hometowns in Palestine. Societal class, rank and structure disappeared overnight in the catastrophe of dispossession and *Nakba* (catastrophe).

Like my parents, most of the camp residents were initially relocated to north Lebanon from the southern borders and from the eastern part of the country. The Lebanese government was intent on removing as many refugees as possible from the new border with Israel. The presence of refugees and their border infiltration became a troublesome affair for the Lebanese authorities. Hitherto, many of the refugees, especially landowners, must have suffered from a "case of denial", as for many years and despite the risk, refugees continued to cross the border illicitly, visiting their destroyed villages and harvesting fruits from their orchards or even bringing soil from their native hometowns. Soil came to symbolize people's eternal connection to the lost land.

I was familiar with many cases where people got stuck on the Israeli side after infiltrating back into their villages, and were perpetually separated from their immediate families in the refugee camps. There were also many other instances where people lost their lives or were captured, imprisoned and later deported by the Israeli army. Soon thereafter, and as refugees started to settle down in the new camps, it became a sign of pride for people to hang up prominently the key to their Palestine home, display a jar full of soil from their hometown, or for landowners to carry with them the registration deed of their misappropriated land.

To transfer them north, the Lebanese government started loading the helpless refugees onto freight trains before dumping them at the final main station near the seaport in the city of Tripoli. The refugees were initially housed in vacated French military barracks, before being divided into two groups: one group to the Nahr el Bared location and another to an old *khan** next to Abu Ali River in the city. The later group was relocated several years later to what became the second Palestinian camp in north Lebanon, Al Badawi. The new camp was established following a devastating flood in Abu Ali River in the late 1950s.

The *Nakba* of 1948 left the Palestinian community penniless and leaderless. The fight for economic survival took precedence in the camp. Politics, however, wasn't very far behind. To fully appreciate the political progression among the refugees, one must first understand the earlier British role of undermining Palestinian nationhood and disenfranchising political leadership. In response to the indigenous opposition to British rule, the Mandate authority adopted official decrees to stifle, kill, imprison and deport national Palestinian leaders.

---

* *Khan* was an Ottoman Empire era hostel type building serving as travel stops for caravans.

In 1935 the British authority killed a regional rebel leader, Al Qassam. In 1936 they imprisoned local leaders accused of participating in the uprising against British rule and protesting the illegal Jewish immigration to Palestine. In 1937 they deported Haj Amin Al Husseini, the Grand Mufti of Palestine. At the same time, the Mandate authority promoted, enabled, and armed local Jewish military groups. As an example, in 1938, the Haganah (the nuclei of the future Israeli army) became an officially recognized paramilitary group assisting the British forces in Palestine. In addition, a British army officer named Orde Charles Wingate went further by convincing his military superiors to create a joint contingent of British and Jewish forces to fight the Palestinians. Wingate personally provided military training to the future Israeli army and was accredited by Moshe Dayan (later Israel's military Chief of Staff and Defense Minister) as the person who "taught us everything we know".[13] Wingate was a Christian Zionist who dedicated his service in the British military to advancing the "fulfillment of Christian prophecy" for the creation of a Jewish state.

Immediately following the *Nakba*, and as the traditional Palestinian leadership was discredited by the catastrophe of 1948, alternative local leadership emerged from exile. New organizations, such as the Pan Arab Nationalist Movement (ANA), established by the late George Habash in 1951 along with other smaller political organizations, found ready recruitment breeding grounds in the camps. These organizations were antecedent of future military groups, where the ANA morphed into the Popular Front for the Liberation of Palestine (PFLP) and others became FATAH. The new guerilla movement led the Palestinian armed struggle and took over the Palestine Liberation Organization (PLO) for decades to come.

A New Life, a New Struggle

In the early 1950s, camp denizens started to improve on their living conditions by constructing rudimentary adobe structures. Natural clay was used as plaster to cover walls of bamboo sticks; natural stones were dug and cemented with clay for new walls. Actually, until our house was destroyed in the summer of 2007,[14] two of the walls in the main bedroom consisted of an adobe wall and another was made of natural stones. I was born in 1958 as the third child in a family of six boys and one girl. I was the first baby born in a room and not in a tent. My first brother, Ghazi, was born in Palestine in 1947. The second brother, Majed, was born in a tent in the refugee camp several years later. I was born after the camp had started to take permanence and people had begun to accept their fate of not returning to their original homes any time soon. I am not quite sure if my birth was a portent of acquiescence in the life of refuge or a blessing that started to provide the family with a sense of stability.

Two years before I was born, UNRWA proposed a plan to replace the tents and the temporary edifices with permanent structures. Because people in the camp held to their enduring longing to go back home, they saw the proposal as an international conspiracy to settle Palestinian refugees in Lebanon and to force them to abandon their original homes in Palestine. In its first spontaneous revolt, the camp's inhabitants vehemently rejected the proposed UNRWA plan. The organizers called on the camp residents to dump and set their tents ablaze in front of UNRWA's offices. UNRWA withdrew its proposal immediately and instead offered help to people who wanted to build permanent structures on an individual basis. As a result, Nahr el Bared ended up being among the most disorganised camp communities in Lebanon. The camp was a cinder-block sprawl where walking through the alleys was challenging even to its inhabitants.

I was born during a sectarian revolt against the Maronite Christian president of Lebanon in 1958. At the time, rumours had it that the president was planning to amend the Lebanese constitution to serve a second term in office. The Lebanese constitution allows the president, who is elected by the parliament, to serve for one single six-year term. The president was supported by the Baghdad Pact, which, in addition to Great Britain, also included at the time the Kingdom of Iraq, Turkey, Iran and Pakistan. On the other side, the Lebanese Pan-Arab rebels, backed by Egyptian president Jamal (Gamal) Abdul Nasser, were determined not to allow President Chamoun to extend his term in office. The American Marines landed in Lebanon in 1958 in support of the embattled Lebanese president and to end the Lebanese Pan-Arab popular revolt. President Chamoun was forced to leave office at the end of his six-year term.

During this upheaval, our home encountered its own mayhem, caused by a six-month-old boy. I was crying endlessly for long periods of time, refused feeding and was turning blue. My father brought home a cow's head to cook for food when he found the infant baby crying hysterically in his mother's arms. My parents suspected a serious problem and decided to go to a makeshift UN clinic at the camp. The doctors at the clinic recommended that it was severe enough that the baby should be taken immediately to the emergency room at the American Mission Hospital in the city of Tripoli. Tripoli, the second largest city in Lebanon, was about ten miles south of the camp.

As luck would have it, my father had just started recently to work as an ambulance driver for the UN. The ambulance was responsible for transporting sick refugees from the two camps in north Lebanon to hospitals and clinics in Tripoli and later in Beirut. Hence my father drove the six-month-old baby to the American hospital in Tripoli himself. I was told that my oldest brother and cousin asked to go along for the ride. When you lived in a refugee camp, riding a car, even an ambulance, was an indulgence you couldn't resist. The ride, however, was not as safe as my brother and cousin may have hoped for or expected. During the short trip from the camp, the ambulance had to pass through a small Lebanese town called Al Miniah, a hotbed of the rebellion against the Lebanese president. In Al Miniah, the ambulance ran into a raging battle between the rebels and the Lebanese army. My father had to manoeuvre the ambulance to dodge flying bullets from all sides. In the back of the ambulance, my mother cloaked the baby with her body as my brother and cousin lay next to her on the ambulance floor.

Finally they arrived at the emergency room of the American hospital, where doctors decided that they had a life-threatening case on their hands, caused by a strangulated groin (inguinal) hernia.

"A hernia?" my mother asked. "How could it be? He is just a baby who hasn't even walked yet." The doctors explained that it might have been present since birth but was strained by crying, which in turn exasperated the condition by restricting the blood flow to the bulged internal organ and the bladder.

My mother recalled that during all that period, the only method of communication for the pained six-month-old baby was crying for help. Today, hernia surgery is conducted as an outpatient procedure with no overnight stay in the hospital. In 1958 and in a refugee camp, the operation was a dangerous procedure that required a stay of several days in the hospital. Fortunately, my mother was able to stay at the hospital and breastfed me through recovery. Considering the period in time, it can be said that my survival was miraculous, for I remember growing up when children's mortality rate was very high. It was a normal event for a mother to die during childbirth and for babies to die in the first months of their lives. Delivering a baby in the camp was a tense procedure full of anticipation and anxiety, for it was seen as a struggle between life and death. At times, life wins with a new baby, and on other occasions, death conquers the process by taking two souls.

Meanwhile, the cow's head was thrown out as it was considered a bad omen and the family swore off eating or cooking cows' heads from that day forward. As a result of that early decision, I never did get to experience tasting a cow's head. The hernia may have been a blessing in disguise.

DETERMINATION

Emotionally, we lived a relatively normal life in the camp. We were cocooned by two parents who were able to make up for life's hardships and shortcomings with genuine affection and total dedication. My paternal grandmother lived with us in the small house. My maternal grandmother and grandfather lived across the alley from our home. Our residence consisted of two bedrooms and a living room. One bedroom was shared by eight of us, five boys, one girl, my mother and grandmother. We all slept on the floor of the approximately 12 x 14 feet of available space. The other smaller bedroom was for my father and oldest brother. The middle living room was used for guests, doing school homework or to gather around the hot charcoal glow during cold winter nights. The house roof was made of tin metal sheeting, which ended up making the house sizzlingly hot during summer and freezing during the cold winter months.

The tin sheeting was secured with long nails embedded in timber battens and held down by the weight of rocks or sand bags on top of the nails. The roof's corrugated tin sheets were about 3 x 6 feet each, and as such they were prone to uplifting in the wind. Unless they were fastidiously secured in place, the tin sheets would fly away during heavy wind storms. One night, during a strong wind and rain storm, our neighbours awoke to find themselves in a roofless room as the heavy winds had yanked the tin sheeting from over their heads. They moved their mattresses into the kitchen and tried to sleep till the morning. During heavy winter storms, I used to enjoy going to sleep to the sound of the rain drumming on the metal sheeting. At times, especially during the first storm of winter, the corrugated sheets would leak. My mother would wake us up in the middle of the night to rearrange the mattresses and to place pails or buckets under the dribbles of rainwater. My parents took turns emptying the containers throughout the night. In the morning, my dad would climb up, throw another corrugated tin or plastic sheet on the roof, and tar it to seal the leaks.

My mother was a stoic and indefatigable individual whose daily travails started early, around 4.30 a.m., with the morning prayer. She then prepared our breakfast while we slept and before starting her long list of household chores. Our breakfast consisted of tea, milk, *zaatar* (spiced oregano), and possibly cheese or eggs. Milk and cheese were distributed by UNRWA and eggs were very affordable as they were produced locally. My favourite breakfast was the homemade cereal, which was made from leftover parched pita crumbs mixed with milk and sugar. Sometimes we substituted milk with hot tea. At that age, I loved hot tea and not just for breakfast but also for lunch as a way to avoid eating a healthy homemade meal.

Another daily task for my mother was washing our clothes and linen. Because we typically had two sets of garments, my mother had to hand-wash our clothes daily. She started by boiling water on firewood in the outside courtyard. Washing clothes was a project that took hours to prepare every day. As an example, the water that we needed to drink, to wash our clothes, clean the hard concrete floor, to shower and to irrigate the edible plants in our small garden all had to be hauled daily from a community public water fountain. In our neighbourhood, we had two public water faucets for about four hundred families. My mother got her turn very early in the morning by placing a water container in a long queue at the fountain. When her turn at the fountain came up, she would start the laborious task of hauling the full containers to replenish the water barrels at home. On each trip, she would place about a seven-gallon bucket on her head and lug a five-gallon pail in her hand. She repeated the trip as many times as necessary until all the water storage containers at home were filled.

Since she used firewood (to save on the cost of fuel) to boil the water, my mother often walked several miles outside the camp to farms and walked along the beach to collect driftwood. Every once in a while she used to take me along with her. On one occasion I was playing close-by, watching my mother work hard pulling and collecting dry bamboo roots and sticks. That day a local farmer found her collecting dry bamboo in close vicinity to the hedge. He became very agitated and started screaming obscenities and told her to leave without the pile of dry wood she had worked so hard to collect. I was very humiliated for my mother. I ran away and started to curse and throw pebbles at the farmer, who caught up with me. My mother had to beg him to let me go: "Please leave my child, please do not hurt him!" Her pleading voice still rings in my ears after so many years. At the end of the day, she had to return empty-handed but for the little scrap of wood we gathered on our walk back home.

Another daily task was making loaves of bread from scratch. My mother mixed the flour and yeast early in the morning and then placed the dough under a warm blanket to hasten the yeast's fermentation. As the dough leavened and was ready for baking, it was worked with a wooden roller, making about forty to fifty loaves of bread, enough for two to three days. She stacked the flat dough in a large circular tray and carried it on her head to the neighbourhood bakery. At the bakery she took her place in line with other women who were doing the same for their families. The baker charged a nominal fee per tray or for a certain number of bread loaves. During the cold winter and when I was very young, I often tagged along with my mother to the baker, seeking to enjoy the warmth of the bakery shop and the smell of fresh baked bread.

Other times my mother built her own fire to bake the bread at home in a *forniah*. This was a handmade outside oven, built by mixing clay with straw. The *forniah* consisted of two compartments, the lower level for the firewood and an upper compartment to place the dough. The *forniah* bread had a much better, more natural taste than the bread baked at the bakery. Whenever my mother baked bread in the *forniah*, it was olive-oil-dipping time. I would ask her to make me a special crunchy loaf of bread to eat by dipping the warm crunchy bread in olive oil. This was in addition to making *manakeesh*, which was made by spreading a mix of oil and *zaatar* on top of the dough, much like a pizza but with different and cheaper ingredients. Eating lots of bread has always been my weakness. For I eat bread with any meal; I even used to joke about eating bread with bread.

On special occasions, my mother used to also bake *saj* bread. This was a paper-thin loaf, approximately eighteen inches in diameter. The *saj* was prepared over a concave steel saucer (similar to a satellite dish) placed on block risers over burning wood. Eating warm *saj* with olive oil was a camp luxury, which I would still prefer today over eating lobster at the best of San Diego restaurants.

The main sources of news and gossip in the camp were while waiting at the public fountain or the bakery. The trip to the public fountain and/or the bakery brought with it news about who was getting married, who was having a child or who was migrating to far-off places, or who was sick and who was dying in the camp. These two places were also where women would get into "cat fights" over their turn for water or to bake the bread. The fights used to get ugly at times, as they could extend to other family members. I remember watching many fights at our neighbourhood fountain. The police were often called in to break up the fights.

With as little as we had in the camp, I have no memory of lacking any of life's pleasures. Philosophically speaking, it is not possible to lack what you have never experienced. In lay terms, you do not miss what you never had. As an example, I remember when we first received electricity at home. Before electricity, a kerosene lantern (*sraj*) was the only light available for us to finish our homework by and to brighten our dark nights. Lying down in the cold bedroom, I used to put myself to sleep while gazing at the *sraj*'s flame in what appeared like a clash between darkness, represented by the intertwined tiny columns of dark smoke, and a tenacious kerosene glow to bring light. I remember many nights waking up with headaches and blackened nostrils from breathing the kerosene smoke while we slept. Then, having electricity meant a 100 per cent improvement to our life and seemed to be a great luxury. However, we did not miss this luxury before we got to experience it. That same philosophy applies to most of life's luxuries and privileges. We did not know what it was like to have a heater in a cold classroom or a fan during a hot summer day. How could we miss having running water at home, hot or cold, when we didn't even know it was possible? Community public latrines were centralized in each neighbourhood, so how could you miss having a bathroom at home when you'd never had one? In short, life was normalized by what we had and not by what was lacking.

Human deprivation can also become a motivating factor for betterment if you choose to work hard, and can be demoralizing in the absence of positive social support. As a refugee child, I did not have a clear prospect of what my future would be like, what school I would attend or what profession I might study for. For the future of the deprived was not guided by their parents' accomplishments or affluence. This reality of life became an advantage, whereby the deprived child was not distracted by the traditional social constraints of defining success in life. As a child, I was not intimidated by success or failure. Can failure bring more deprivation? Or is it possible to lose what you do not have? Failure in the camp was to live another day under the same dreadful conditions, while success was defined by the ability to survive yet another day in the same appalling environment. In an ironic way, success and failure had a congruent tinge inside the camp. For the real gratifying triumph was in the individual's faculty to move on and to eventually help sustain decent life for those who remained in the land of purgatory, otherwise known as the camp.

Early in life, children in the camp were made to realize that they were the only assets for their parents' future. In other words, children at a young age understood very well their social obligations toward securing a decent life for their parents when they advanced in age. Hence, parents worked hard to protect their assets and offspring. By nature, the camp environment promoted independent children who could count only on their parents' emotional support. As such, the camp was a supportive environment where "birds" were encouraged to soar far from the flock, yet find it safe to go back to the tree.

Because of the lack of available options, children were taught obliquely that their only hope for a decent life was in higher education or a skilled trade. Life betterment in the camp meant the need to migrate to far places seeking education, work or job training to master a skilled trade. One must understand that Palestinian refugees, despite being long-term residents or even born in Lebanon, were forbidden by government regulations to work or practise in more than seventy trades. Lebanese-born Palestinians were considered to be refugees and were not granted any residency rights. Official Lebanese government trade institutions and higher education were closed to Palestinians. Skilled trade mastery was only available inside the camps and later through UN-established institutions. With limited opportunities within the camps, emigration from Lebanon was almost the only option available for economic advancement.

Since migration was a supply and demand industry, the older generation steered the younger generation to develop occupational skills for the regional and to a lesser extent for the global migrant market. Typically, technical learning such as engineering was the most desired by parents, as it was much easier for engineers to land jobs and to migrate to the new growing oil economies in the region. The move toward technical learning in the camp, however, represented a paradigm shift, as in the 1950s and early 1960s the regional migrant market demand was for school teachers. During that period, the camp produced a large number of school teachers who were able to find jobs in Saudi Arabia and other oil-producing countries in the Gulf region.

My parents were very keen on and passionate about education, even though neither had ever had an opportunity to go to school. I wondered sometimes if my parents' lack of education was the impetus for their passion for learning. Their motivation was possibly found by observing the positive impact of schooling on the lives of educated individuals.

When I attended high school in the city of Tripoli, and to save on the cost of transportation, my dad used to pick me up in the UNRWA ambulance he drove for his work. Next to his seat in the ambulance, I would always find the daily newspaper which my dad purchased so I could read him the headlines. I relished those precious moments on the short ride home.

Three years later, while attending college in Houston, Texas, I worked at a self-service gas station during the Iranian turmoil and the ensuing oil crises in 1979. During that period, service stations received limited allocations of gas and used to close shop early. One day, around 2.30, in the afternoon, I hung up the closed sign on the window of the self-service station and was closing my books for the day when an older African-American man parked his car and tried to pump gas. He looked at me and was baffled as to why the pump was not filling the tank. From inside the small kiosk, I pointed at the closed sign. The gentleman ignored the sign and kept trying to pump gas while I kept pointing at the "We Are Closed" sign, but to no avail.

I got very agitated and shouted over the microphone: "Can't you see the sign?"

He seemed confused, came closer to the kiosk and wondered, "Why I can't pump gas?"

I said in an irritated tone, "Read the sign, we are closed."

He looked at me and said, "I can't read."

His response was like splashing freezing water on my face. I was greatly embarrassed and humbled by the incident.

I was ashamed because I immediately remembered when my father used to ask me to read him the headlines from the newspaper. I was ashamed because it might not have been this poor person's fault that he couldn't read. I was embarrassed because I recognized that my own dad would have been equally challenged had he been in the exact same position. I realized that anyone can be a victim of their circumstance.

Notes

--

1 Clevland, William L., *A Hisory of the Modern Middle East*, Second Edition (Boulder, Colorado: Simon Fraser University West View Press, 2000), p. 248.

2 Schoenman, R., *The Hidden History of Zionism* (Santa Barbara, California: Veritas Press, 1988).

3 Khalidi, W., *From Haven to Conquest: Readings in Zionism and the Palestine Problem until 1948* (Washington, DC: Institute for Palestine Studies, 1987).

4 Morris, B., *The Birth of the Palestinian Refugee Problem Revisited* (Cambridge: Cambridge University Press, 2004).

5 12th House, "Jewish National Fund, Founded December 29, 1901", at http://www.hagshama.org.il/en/resources/view.asp?id=1050, retrieved 5 January 2007.

6 http://www.jnf.org/support/tree-planting-center/, retrieved April 2009.

7 Kadman, Noga, *Erased from Space and Consciousness, Depopulated Palestinian Villages in the Israeli-Zionist Discourse* (Master's thesis in Peace and Development Studies, Department of Peace and Development Research, Goteborg University, November 2001).

8 Stern, Yoav, *Haaretz*, 2 March 2008.

9 http://www.mideastweb.org/unscop1947.htm, retrieved May 2008.

10 Masalha, Nur, *Expulsion of the Palestinians: The Concept of Transfer in Zionist Political Thought* (Washington, DC: Institute for Palestine Studies, 1992), p. 176.

11 For more information on the Zionist military operations, refer to Pappé, Ilan, *The Ethnic Cleansing of Palestine* (Oxford: Oneworld

Publications, 2006), and Masalha, Nur, *Expulsion of the Palestinians: The Concept of Transfer in Zionist Political Thought* (Washington, DC: Institute for Palestine Studies, 1992).

12 For detailed accounts and a list of the destroyed Palestinian villages visit http://www.palestineremembered.com/index.html.

13 http:/en.wikipedia.org/wiki/orde_Wingate, retrieved May 2008.

14 The camp was completely destroyed in the summer of 2007 by the Lebanese army. For the story of the camp destruction, see Chapter 9.

2

Life in the Camp

—-—

First School

During my early childhood, I never experienced the joy of having a book read to me at bedtime. My parents would have loved to have done so if only they could read. In fact, the first book read in my bed was by me. However, the lack of bed-time reading was made up for by the cold nights spent as a family cuddled in blankets on our mattresses, or around the amber charcoal fire with elderly neighbors visiting my grandma. During those gatherings, we would plead with our visitors to share stories with us. Almost always they did. Some were fictitious tales and some were anecdotal about their life in Palestine, but we enjoyed them equally.

Before starting elementary school, I attended a UN-sponsored preschool. The preschool was financed by a grant from the United Nations Children's Fund (UNICEF) through UNRWA. The camp had one class of about thirty preschool children. The teacher happened to be our neighbor; her name was Ms Warda or "Flower" in English. Ms Warda was a nice-looking, tall and skinny girl. One day, Ms Warda wore a short skirt while supervising and playing with us at the playground. She took turns with us on the swing and I could not help noticing her exposed beautiful legs as she swung. I must have thought myself to be invisible as I wrapped myself around a steel post and started to stare at her bare legs. As the swing went higher, Ms Warda revealed more of her slender legs and the fluttering skirt began to expose her alluring black briefs. Ms Warda noticed me gazing and said: "Jamal, mind your eyes." Even though that was all she said, I was deeply embarrassed and the detail of that event was forever engraved in my memory.

The camp also had a UN-managed elementary and middle school. The elementary and middle school pupils were all Palestinian refugees from historical northern Palestine. To attend high school, pupils had to travel to the city of Tripoli and enroll in either private or public schools with mixed classes of Palestinians and Lebanese pupils.

At a very young age I was well aware of my identity as a Palestinian refugee residing in another country. The pupils in the classroom were usually identified by their last names or by the name of their original village in Palestine. The camp was unofficially divided between Palestinian villages. Residents from the village of Saffuriyya lived in the upper side of the camp, villagers from the town of Sa'sa' settled across the main street, the village of Damoon inhabited part of the shoreline, and so on. Likewise, early in the school year, the classrooms were also informally sectionalized by the name of the village. This continued until the teacher forced the pupils to change seats, based on their height. Each classroom had as many as fifty pupils. The short pupils sat at the front and the taller children sat at the back. It was a real advantage for the shorter pupils to be seated at the front, which likely resulted in getting more attention from teachers, especially in the large classrooms. And that possibly explained the reason why the shortest pupils usually got the better grades in the class. In later years, and as pupils from different villages became friends, kids abandoned their village sections and sat next to their new friends.

I started elementary schooling in the fall of 1964. I must have had the best first-grade teacher anyone could wish for in their early childhood education. His name was Mr Taib, which translates as "Mr Tasty" in English! Mr Taib was devoted to his pupils' learning. Even on his small monthly salary, he occasionally handed out monetary rewards to encourage good class performance. One afternoon he was pleased with the class and rewarded each child with 10 Lebanese pennies, which must have amounted to more than the daily allowance, if any, for most of the pupils. Unbeknown to him, Mr Taib had a great positive influence on my learning that would last a lifetime.

CHILD ALLOWANCE

Kids in the camp were very creative in identifying resources to gain or supplement their spending money. In the camp it was even more important to find supplemental sources, as the daily allowance was very small, if any at all. One way of supplementing our income was to sell rationed powdered milk handed out by UNRWA. The UN organization distributed a daily milk ration to families with young children. When milk was in surplus or not needed at home, we sold the milk to wholesale buyers waiting just outside the UN agency distribution center. A portion of the money was given to the child who went to the trouble of collecting the milk ration.

Other financial supplemental ventures required cooperation and teamwork between kids. These included collecting and selling discarded animal bones from the dump site, illegally digging up sand from the shoreline to sell to construction contractors and selling scrap brass to metal dealers.

The dump site for the camp was located in our neighborhood along the coastline. Butchers discarded the bones from cows and sheep at the site daily. One day we noticed a stranger with a mule and cart collecting bones from the dump site. When we inquired, he told us that the collected bones were sold as raw material to manufacturers in Tripoli to make service plates and cups. We negotiated a deal with him to collect, pile and load the bones weekly for a fee. He agreed to pay us 35 Lebanese pennies weekly for a full load. A group of us nine-year-olds created a small business enterprise: a number of us were to collect the bones and another group was responsible for filling the cart each Friday. The two groups reversed roles every week or so. After the man paid us every week, on his way to Tripoli, he took us for a free ride to the nearby Lebanese village of Al Miniah to buy fishing materials and to pick free fruit.

Digging up sand and aggregate as building material for concrete mix was another of our ventures, even though it was against the law to dig up or sell sand and aggregate from public beaches. Nevertheless, as the construction contractors needed the material, we were ready to deliver for a fee. The buyers furnished picks and shovels for a group of us to start working early in the morning during low tide, to pile the sand above the tide line. To avoid being discovered and caught by the Lebanese police, we hid the heap behind natural barriers, or loaded it very early in the morning. We charged about

1.25 Lebanese pounds (about 50 cents at the time) to load a small trailer of about ½ m³ (⅔ cubic yards). The amount we were paid for the sand and aggregate was higher than all of our other projects. It was physically very demanding work for nine- or ten-year-old children. This type of work was usually done at the weekend and mostly during the long summer break when construction activities were at their peak.

Another supplemental income source was collecting old and discarded electric wires from the trash dump. We stripped the discarded electric wires and sold the copper to scrap-metal buyers. It was sold by weight. At times, to make an extra penny, we tried to cheat the dealer by wrapping the stripped copper wires around a pebble to make it heavier, hence getting a higher fee. Scrap-metal buyers used to watch out for these tricks. When you were discovered, you first lost your credit of trust and then you were forced to unwind the wire, remove the stone and rewrap the copper again.

This venture became a dangerous business enterprise when some of the children went from collecting discarded electric wire to salvaging live electric wire knocked down after Israeli air raids on the camp. After each Israeli military raid or battle in the camp, overhead high tension electric wires fell over the damaged areas. Boys moved in soon after the raid, before the arrival of the power company crew, to collect the fallen power lines. Collecting high tension electric wires earned faster rewards as the power cables were thick, weighed more, and there was no insulation to be stripped off. However, there were instances when kids accidentally handled live wires lying on the ground that resulted in serious injuries or even death in some cases.

Farm labor was yet another source of income. Whenever I tried to work on a farm, I faced stern opposition at home, as my father wanted me to focus on my schooling. Nevertheless, by the age of thirteen I had on occasions lined up in the early morning with farm laborers to ride a truck to the fields north of the camp. At other times, I was able to convince my mother to allow me to go with other kids to pick up the leftover harvest of peanuts and potatoes. After farmers finished harvesting their peanut and potato crops, we would go and pick what they had failed to or were unable to pick up from their farms. I went several times to harvest potatoes, but much less often to pick up peanuts. This was because harvesting peanuts was harder work and I wasn't successful most of the time in getting enough peanuts to cover the transportation cost. In contrast, since the size of a potato was larger, I was able to bring enough potatoes home to make it worthwhile. For the potato pick, we left before sunrise with someone who was familiar with the location of the already harvested farms. As we arrived at the field, we lined up in a straight line with a hoe, and started to plow the hard soil to unearth leftover potatoes. Farmers for the most part didn't mind having people coming to pick the extra crops from the ground since this resulted in tilling the soil and indirectly prepared it for the next planting season. Digging for leftover potatoes was hard work. Many times we spent hours before finding out that the field had already been dug once before by others. Then we had to move on to look for another field. The potato season was at the end of summer, the sun was hot and the soil was very dry. We got lucky at times, arriving at farms soon after the soil had been mechanically ploughed by the farmers. At that point, the soil was softer to dig or even at times the head of potatoes were brought to the surface by the mechanical plow. Instead of digging the hard soil, we could walk around and collect the surfaced potatoes. Farmers did not mind us doing this either, as we were clearing the fields of potential seeds that could interfere with their seasonal planting.

FUN YEARS

I enjoyed my life as a child except for the long
the first seven years of schooling. Classes ran __
until 12.20; then we had a long lunch break until 2 p.m. and
back to school until 4.20 in the afternoon. Before we had
electricity at home, we hurried up to finish our homework
during the remaining daylight hours to avoid studying under
the dim *sraj* or kerosene light.

We enjoyed long summer breaks from about 15 June to
almost 15 September. In the first week of school, unknown
to our parents, a group of us skipped the afternoon classes to
spend more time on the beach. The teachers were not very
strict during the first week, and we wanted to extend our
summer break. The Mediterranean was typically at its best
during the months of August and September; beautiful, calm,
blue and serene. As the weather and water started to cool down
in the September and October months, the Mediterranean
rock crab began to spawn in shallow water. Rock crabs are
very similar to stone crabs, but they're smaller and have a
rougher outer shell. Our favorite pastime was to walk the
shorelines searching for crabs under rocks during low tide. To
avoid being nipped by their sharp claws, we slipped our hands
from behind (a blind spot for the crabs) to grab the claws
tight. The crab's nip was severe and excruciating, but it was
very weak and almost incapable of unlocking the claws when
held shut. At times, we ripped the claws off and let the crab
go, at other times we kept the whole crab. Before sundown,
we would collect dry wood to start a small fire for freshly
barbequed crab meat.

In addition to catching crabs, I loved fishing, and trapping
and hunting birds. Trapping was the first level in bird-catching
and hunting. To fool the poor bird, we covered the trap with
light sand and tied a corn worm to a trigger mechanism,

releasing the trap when the bird attempted to eat the worm. The bird trap was very similar to the mousetrap used at home, but not as strong. To catch the bird alive, we hid close by, and ran quickly to release the bird from the trap.

The second intermediate hunting level was the sling shot. Although one boy was very good at knocking his target with the sling shot, I wasn't. The next level was a muzzle-loading rifle and BB guns. When I was ten, I bought illicitly (from my parents) a muzzle-loading rifle for hunting birds. To make a cartridge, the muzzle-loader is filled first with granular gun powder, followed by a small sheet of paper pressed down with a ramrod to compact the powder. The piece of paper is inserted as a divider and to provide uniform compaction for the powder. Then metal pellets are inserted, followed by another piece of paper to ram the pellets and the powder together, thereby creating an impromptu shooting cartridge. A small capsule was then affixed to a special slot at the end of the barrel to produce a spark. The spark was produced by releasing the trigger igniting the powder.

The muzzle-loading rifle was unsafe in its own right. Occasionally, and to produce stronger shot, I would overload the barrel with extra powder, which resulted at times in blowing up the muzzle or caused a reverse fire by launching the cap backward at the end of the gun barrel. My typical muzzle-loading gun was wrapped with wires to keep the barrel securely attached to the wood frame. As my dad loved to own guns, he always had a shotgun at home, which was later upgraded to an automatic military machine gun, soon after the PLO moved into the camp. When I turned sixteen, my father allowed me to borrow his shotgun to hunt for larger migratory birds. In addition to native birds, hunting the migrating starlings was an annual ritual that started mid-autumn. In the late afternoon, flocks of starlings flew past the camp. Along with other hunters, I took a spot by the river, waiting for the flocks of the passing starlings. Depending on the distance and how sparse the flock was, a lucky hunter could hit many birds with one shot. Hunters with double barrels were at an advantage as, following the first shot, the terrified starlings would pack together, and then the second shot was usually successful in achieving multiple kills. Other hunting periods were mostly during severe cold storms when Lebanon was invaded by throngs of sundry migratory birds from Europe. Looking back now, if there was any possible excuse for killing those helpless birds, I always hunted for food and never wasted my catch.

For fishing, I saved money or drew on my supplemental income to buy a fishing line and a hook. I made a fishing rod from bamboo-like reeds, used a pebble for weight and a bottle cork for a float. My favorite place for fishing was across the river just outside the camp on a rocky beach. We used small baby shrimp captured from the tide pool for bait. I didn't necessarily catch much fish, but it was a great pastime during off-school days. The sea was very rich with all kinds of marine life, exotic fish and plants. Things changed quickly, however, when fishing by dynamite became the new prevalent method for professional and amateur fishermen alike. I will come back to fishing with dynamite later on in this chapter.

The Mediterranean was not always friendly. High waves and flooding during heavy storms could result in disaster and death. On one occasion, during a strong winter sea storm, a group of us was enjoying the heavy surf. We shared a superstitious belief that the sea, like the ox, gets agitated and waves become larger if flaunted with something red. During a storm with heavy surge, we decided to tease the sea, or so we thought, by putting on red clothing and running into the surf after the receding water and then running back trying to beat the incoming waves before they broke on the beach. However, one day a child ran out of luck as the wave broke around a concrete structure and swept the little kid back into the "belly" of the flail. The kid wasn't a very good swimmer, but even if he had been, the waves were so strong he didn't stand a chance. He was swallowed by the waves and disappeared inside the white foam. It was several days before his body was finally washed ashore, miles away from the camp.

I admired and loved the Mediterranean unconditionally. I loved it when it was calm, and equally when it got infuriated. The Mediterranean presented unmatched beauty with its sparkling water when peaceful, and demanded special respect for its majestic power when fuming.

THE KILLING OF A SEA

I have pleasant summer memories of standing on the shoreline and looking into the crystal clear water to watch schools of fish, octopus, squid and crab. When I became a good swimmer, I enjoyed snorkeling and diving with eels amid the beautiful reef. As a young child, I felt as if I owned a piece of the Mediterranean, because of the great deal of time I'd spent swimming and fishing.

In the late 1960s, as the central Lebanese government was weakened, fishing by dynamite explosive provided an immediate reward for those hoping to get a fast catch. Fishing by dynamite contributed to the killing of the Mediterranean and destroying its natural resources in the local area. Like war bombs that do not distinguish between civilians and the military, fishing by explosives did not discriminate between small and large fish. Introducing dynamite as a fishing method was devastating to the fish population and to the overall marine ecology. It ended up eradicating seaweed and other important sources of food for marine life. I must confess that I too experimented with this type of illegal fishing when I was as young as ten years old. I know of many people who lost their hands and/or hearing, and some were even killed by premature explosions. It is true that the economic hardship in the camp contributed to the use of this fishing method to achieve faster rewards, but by wanting more, we killed it all. Fishing by explosive is analogous to the story of the Golden Goose. The Golden Goose laid a golden egg every day. This went on until the owners got greedy and decided to kill the goose to get all the hidden eggs at once. The Mediterranean was killed to catch more fish. When the goose was killed, it wasn't able to produce more golden eggs and when the Mediterranean was "killed", fish became very sparse.

While fishing by explosive was an immediate cause for killing the Mediterranean in the vicinity of the Lebanese shores, one must remember that other pollutant factors contributed greatly to its overall environmental degradation. According to a study published by the World Health Organization (WHO) in 1990:

> 80–85% of the total amount of pollutants entering the Mediterranean comes from land-based sources. Municipal wastes from coastal population centres, including tourist complexes, are discharged directly into the sea, very largely without having been treated. Industrial wastes may be discharged in a similar manner or may reach the sea from inland locations through rivers, canals, and the atmosphere. The intensification and mechanization of agriculture have led to the increased use of pesticides and fertilizers, a certain proportion of which reaches the sea indirectly through rivers and the atmosphere.

I am not an environmentalist, but my own experience with the destruction of the Mediterranean was a tough lesson in ecology. Later in life, as I became a professional civil engineer and had to deal with environmentalists on engineering projects, I must acknowledge that even when it seemed as if the environmentalists were unreasonable in interpreting or in applying environmental regulations on projects, I would take a step back and remember what happened to the Mediterranean. My own life experience taught me that I would rather deal with the "headaches" of environmentalists than live to see yet another natural resource destroyed by reckless and selfish human activities.

MIDDLE SCHOOL

To graduate from the sixth grade and to move up to the seventh grade (middle school), students in Lebanon had to first obtain a formal government certificate. My grandmother, who died a year earlier, used to read me her rose beads to foretell the results of the upcoming sixth grade test. I was the second son to become eligible to take the exam. My oldest brother, Ghazi, had passed the exam several years earlier; my other older brother, Majed, had to drop out of school after the fifth grade to learn a trade. I was next in line. The standard middle school entrance test is scheduled the same day throughout Lebanon. Our school took the exam at a middle school named Al Mea'tain in the city of Tripoli. Each test room had two proctors to distribute the exams and to collect the papers when finished. The Arabic writing composition part of the test consisted of writing on the independence of Lebanon and describing the hoisting of the Lebanese flag in celebrating the event. While schools in the camp observed the Lebanese Independence Day as a holiday, we never held a formal celebration, and there was no Lebanese flag flown at our school. It was hard for children from our school to describe an event that was not celebrated or to describe an object that wasn't part of our school's life. The only way a Palestinian pupil from the camp could write about such a topic was to write from his or her imagination. Many kids from the camp got stuck on the composition topic and failed to write much on the subject. I also know of some kids who wrote about and described the *Palestinian* flag. As a result, many of these kids failed the exam and had to drop out of school or repeat sixth grade all over again.

I for one developed a two-part strategy: firstly, considering the growing anti-Palestinian right-wing movement in Lebanon, I was afraid that an anti-Palestinian grader might not be objective, knowing that the test-taker was a Palestinian refugee. To elaborate on this important point, I must reflect on the interminable inner feelings of the Palestinian refugees as being not welcomed or accepted in the host country. For one, I always felt like an outsider, apart from when I was inside the camp. The camp was a "prototype" of Palestine in another land. It was safe to be with other refugees. Whether those feelings of being unwanted reflected the reality of life or were just part of a psychosomatic self-torment, these beliefs were true to me and have shaped my own perception toward life outside the camp.

Accordingly, I decided to write in such a way that not even the slightest hint of my identity as a Palestinian refugee was revealed to the grader. Secondly, I relied on the best of my imagination to describe an event I'd never actually witnessed. Luckily, earlier in the school year, our class had worked on an Arabic writing composition to describe the street beggar. One pupil wrote a superb story describing the beggar and his clothing. The teacher asked the pupil to read his essay to the class. In addition to providing an overall description of the bigger state, the fellow classmate described how the beggar's clothing was quilted in dissimilar colorful pieces that made him look like the multi-colored field plots of Lebanon's Beqaa farming valley. I borrowed the idea and used an analogous metaphor to describe the hoisting of the Lebanese flag at my school. Among other things, I wrote how we stood to attention as the school principal raised the Lebanese flag, and went on to describe the colors of the flag as a white middle stripe to symbolize Lebanon's ice cap mountains, framed by two red stripes to signify our sacrifice, and decorated by a beautiful green cedar tree in the center to denote the deep-rooted history of Lebanon.

The English spelling portion of the exam was a little easier. For this test period, two teachers came to dictate an English paragraph. As the words were read, one of the proctors also spelled out loud the hard-to-spell words! It was confusing at first and it took me a while to realize that the teacher was giving out the vocabulary spelling each time he dictated a difficult word. Of course he wasn't supposed to, but he must have held an unconventional view toward those tests and wanted to beat the system in his own way. I still remember the word "succeed" as being one of those tough dictation words in the test. I must admit that the teacher may have helped me pass the English spelling test, as I was then a bad speller, and remain one today.

Once the official exam results were compiled, local newspapers published the names of successful students. About a month after the exam, I was awakened to a famous song rejoicing the success in the final school exams. The radio broadcaster announced that the names of students passing the middle school test were published in the morning paper. Like other kids and interested parents, I went running to the souk (market) looking for the newspaper. A large crowd of parents and hopeful pupils alike were gathered around a person reading the successful names aloud. I waited to hear my name but to no avail. When the person was done reading, I asked to borrow the paper. He enquired about my name and then said that I had passed. To my elation, he showed me my name in the paper. I was euphoric, and ran back home to share the news with my mother who was waiting with great anticipation. As was traditional, following the news, my mother asked my little brother to pass candy around to the neighborhood's children to the sound of music and the famous song blasting from the radio. My mom was ecstatic to see her son advancing to middle school. At that joyful moment, I wished my grandmother was alive, for she too would have been very happy. I couldn't wait for my father to come home from Beirut to share the good news. Just after 2 p.m., I heard him by the outside door. I went running to open the door, but he already knew. He hugged me and gave me a kiss. My father didn't kiss me for just anything, and that wasn't just a kiss from Dad, it was *the* kiss. I asked him how he found out about the results since he couldn't read. He told me that after buying the paper, he had asked someone to look for the name. When it was found, my dad had thanked him and told him that it was his son's name.

FIRST LOVE, CAMP STYLE

The following September I moved into middle school. In elementary school we had separate boys' and girls' classes. In the middle school the classes were co-ed. There were over thirty boys and about twelve girls in each class. Most of the girls used to quit school after the sixth grade, either for not passing the middle school entrance exam or to stay at home and help their mothers with their domestic work, in essence, to prepare young girls to become "good" wives. Those days, a good wife was measured not by her education but by being *ma'dali* or well-rounded and dexterous in her household duties. More importantly, education at the time seemed to be a limited investment and families were predisposed to invest in boys, as the future men were expected to take care of their elderly parents. However, and to the disillusionment of many elderly parents, the pay off on the "investment" sometimes didn't necessarily materialize in a positive payback.

I was about twelve or thirteen years old when I started middle school. I am not quite sure whether it was my hormones or the mixed classes that prompted it, but I soon started to develop a healthy interest in members of the opposite sex. I began to exhibit the typical signs of a teenager, taking better care of my looks, combing my hair more often and dressing up more neatly. My good school friend and I had our eyes on the same girl. Somehow it didn't bother either of us. It wasn't really falling love *per se*; it was more like a crush or fascination with the most attractive girl in the seventh grade. Since her home was located by the asphalt road inside the camp, I always found an excuse to walk by. To get outside, she also found a reason to sweep in front of the house. We never talked or touched each other. We only exchanged glinting smiles and winks. I knew she was attracted to me too. Even though there was a public fountain closer to her house, she used to come to the far-off fountain in our neighborhood. It was part of the daily chores for women in the camp to haul drinking water to fill their storage tanks at home. Like the other *ma'dali* girls in the camp, after school she did the same at our neighborhood fountain. When she started her laborious trips with a pail over her head and a bucket in her hand, I also started strolling down the same alley in the opposite direction. She made about ten to fifteen trips back and forth carrying water, and I made the same number of trips walking back and forth waiting to take a glimpse of her coy smile or to get a wink from her dazzling eyes. She seemed too tall with a water tank extended over her head. To balance it on the top, the poor girl had to maintain a stiff neck and could only look straight ahead. It was difficult to turn her face sideways, up or down. To catch my eye to the side while maintaining her posture, she had to strain her eyes looking sideways to wink back or to smile. It wasn't easy in our culture those days for young teenagers to talk in the open. I never talked to her to express my feelings. I would have been too scared considering that her father and my dad were good friends.

We were not, however, exclusive in our "wink relationship" as I was able to wink and exchange smiles with other girls too. I am sure she did with other boys too. Nonetheless, she was the only girl with whom I felt something special.

About two years later, she was engaged to someone from the Beirut area. Her grandfather, who lived in a camp near Beirut, arranged for the engagement and her dad either obliged or was also in a hurry to get her married. There was no question that she did not have any hope that our infatuation would develop into something more concrete in the future. I still had many years before finishing school. She accepted the husband and soon they got married and moved to Beirut. I don't remember seeing her again after moving from the camp. I found out when I was attending college in the United States that her husband had been killed, and shortly before that her younger brother had put a gun to his head and killed himself. With her husband's death she lost everything to his family, including her children. She had no place to go but to move back "to the tree" to live with her parents. An older widower from the camp then asked for her hand in matrimony. Her father was again in a rush to get rid of her into another marriage. She married the widower who was, at the time, a bit of a ruffian, a drinker and a gambler.

I ran into her once or twice in the camp during my visits many years later. She looked sad. We exchanged a restrained glimpse, but without the smile or the wink. I really doubt she could smile the way she had when our eyes met in that alley. I don't think I could smile or wink that way either.

I was a novice fourteen-year-old who was trying to adjust to middle school years and succumb to the teenage rebellion within. I flirted with other girls as well, but the story was almost always the same, they got married and moved on with their life. While parents in the camp loved their children equally, they were almost always in a rush to marry off their daughters. There was an unspoken cultural dogma in the camp, where girls were perceived as an economic burden for their families, while boys were born with the promise of future economic relief for their parents. In the absence of any governmental social system like a pension scheme, an income-earning progeny, typically male, brought the promise of providing for his elderly parents in their later years. I am not sure though, if people married their daughters purely out of economic necessity or just as part of the social order. Girls typically got married by the age of sixteen to someone in his early twenties who had mastered a work skill, to a migrant in a far-off place or to someone who'd been earning money for several years after leaving school at a young age. The "social order" has changed considerably since then, as "girls" have proven to be as much or even more capable of providing not just for the social economic security net, but more importantly for the emotional needs of the elderly parents in their later years.

SWIMMING WITH THE SHARKS

The last year of middle school was not very eventful. I continued to daydream in the classroom about a place far, far away from the purgatory of life in the camp. Whenever I saved enough money, I went to Tripoli, seeking a transitory escape into a movie theater to watch a new release of an Egyptian motion picture. At the same time, the sectarian strife in Lebanon was slowly simmering in all aspects of daily Lebanese life.

Leading into the school year, I started to work as a part-time fisherman. Almost every afternoon, I went with two brothers to borrow a rowing boat for dynamite fishing. After covering the cost of the dynamite, the yield was split four ways. Each of us got one share and the owner of the boat got the boat's share. I was a good diver who could hold his breath for a long time without an oxygen tank or other breathing apparatus. This came in useful when diving deep to collect the dead fish from the sea bed. When killing fish by dynamite became the prevailing fishing method, small six-foot sharks also became rampant at the fishing locations. Sharks were instinctively smart animals, associating water explosions with dead fish. The sound of a dynamite blast travels far underwater. The power and frequency of detonations indicated to the sharks the size of the dead fish. With multiple simultaneous explosions at different sites, sharks were able to decipher where to go first. Actually, some fishermen used to keep the size and number of dynamite blasts to a minimum, hoping to fool the sharks. After the initial kill, fishermen entered into a race against time to collect as much of their catch as possible before the arrival of sharks. While dynamite fishing was an effective killing system, sharks were also efficient gobbling machines competing for their kill. Unless exploded over their heads, sharks were not affected by dynamite blasts.

It was typical for fishermen to ask me to help them collect the fish before the arrival of sharks. Most fishermen were not afraid of sharks and used to compete directly in collecting the fish, but not me. I was still terrified seeing the shark fin rising above the water surface or swimming in the water under me. Whenever I saw sharks in the water, I used to either swim back to the shore or jump into the boat.

One day, I was with friends in a car driving north of the camp when we noticed a school of yellowtail fish spattering water on the surface about 3,000 feet from the beach. The driver parked the car, put on his snorkel, took two sticks of dynamite and started to swim toward the school of fish. Once near the spattering fish, he threw the dynamite and started to swim backwards and away from the explosion. After the blast, he called on us to come and help collect the dead fish. Since he knew of my trepidation when it came to sharks, I suspect he didn't want me to find out about the presence of sharks in the area. For that reason he had me carry a holding net to keep the catch on the surface while they dived to collect the fish from the sea floor. My job was to swim to the divers as they came up with their yield. To keep an eye on the divers, I took a peek through my snorkels and saw lots of fish on the floor bed. A minute later, and after lifting my head up for some air and to gather the fish from the divers, I peeped again and noticed the dead fish were fast disappearing. I went toward the divers and submerged my snorkel back in the water, where I saw a large shark gulping the dead fish faster than the divers could collect them. I immediately raised my head and screamed at my friends to tell them that sharks were in the water. They told me they knew. I said I was leaving. They beseeched me to stay a little longer. I hesitated, despite being an easy target for the sharks while holding a large net full of bloodied, dead fish! Then, before I got a chance to start swimming away, a medium-sized shark started to encircle me. The shark's sharp gazing blue eye was fixed on me as it swam in a shrinking ring in the murky water. It moved slowly at first and then abruptly speeded up. At that stage it was my life or the bloody fish in the net. I decided to swim for my life. I threw the net in the water and started to swim away backward while my head was still in the water looking at the fast-moving shark. As the fish net parachuted slowly toward the sea bottom, the shark swiftly stopped gyrating and made a quick short turn toward the falling fish. In very short seconds, the shark guzzled all the fish that had taken us at least twenty minutes to collect. Needless to say, my friends were mad, but I am not sure if they were mad at me for releasing the fish or at the unruly shark. We just did not talk about it.

MEMORIES PASSED ON

After fishing, as the warm sun started to dwindle during late summer days, we used to head to the green grass area by the El Bared "Cold" river. There were no parks or designated areas for kids or for families in the camp. The natural green setting by the river instantly became a nice play- and meeting-area for young and old alike. About the same time, a group of older men also gathered almost every day after their afternoon prayer, forming a circle to talk about life in general. Almost always, they managed to have time to reminisce about their past lives in their homes before 1948. These were older men in their late sixties and early seventies. Along with other kids, I enjoyed sneaking next to the group to listen to their stories about Palestine. The older men were mostly from small towns and villages known for their farms, horses and orchards. Members in the group challenged each other as to who had the oldest building or tree in their village. One would swear that they had olive-producing trees as old as an-nabi Isa (the Prophet Jesus). Another person interrupted the discussion to remind the group of the colossal oak tree antedating the Messiah in the center of their town. Others joined in to talk about the umpteen grape vines or prolific fig trees. Then someone interjected to tell the group about his village's priceless wood crafts made from old olive or almond trees that were exported to North and South America. And then, and out of the blue, the discussion might take a sharp turn as they started sharing accounts about massacres and the terror of Zionist groups. Their memories became more politically didactic when describing the British role in arming the Zionists and undermining the native population. "The British were entrusted with Palestine by the League of Nations," one person said, "and instead of protecting Palestine, England turned it over to the European Jews." "Wasn't that what they did in America and Australia?" another person asked. The discussion would go on until dusk and it was time for their evening prayer. For these older men, it was a nostalgic time and a cathartic regular session; for us kids it was stories about the homeland we knew only in our imagination and through the stories passed on from one generation to the next. About four years later, this circle was broken when one member of the group was killed by an Israeli cluster bomb in the same area.

3

Revolution and Political Evolution

——

As discussed in an earlier chapter, I was fully aware at a very young age of my predicament as a victim of political injustice. This experience helped me to become more politically conscious of my environment.

Political injustice or socio-economic oppression does not necessarily translate to political awareness. While it may lead to the development of a keen interest in political justice, it can on the other hand also lead to resignation and apathy in inertly self-defeated communities. All the same, the overall environment has the greatest impact on the social and political development of individuals.

My political evolution initially started when we made a habit of listening to news broadcasts. My father bought a radio soon after settling at the camp and was an avid listener to programs like the BBC Arabic news. Having no option but to be exposed to the audio broadcast in the small house, the daily news became an important source for my subtle and subconscious political upbringing. At a very young age, I developed a great interest in an educational BBC program that was aired at 6.45 a.m. Lebanon time. It was usual for my father to turn on his radio at 6.00 a.m. for the first morning news and keep it running to catch the second airing at 7.00 a.m. At 6.45 a.m., I had to listen by default to a program called *Between the Questioner and the Answerer*. The radio show used to respond to questions submitted by listeners throughout the Arabic-speaking world. Questions varied from historical and financial to current political events.

It is important to point out that people like my dad were addicted to news radio as the only contact with the outside world from within the isolated camp. Residents were veritably, alas fallaciously, awaiting the call announcing their return to their homes in Palestine. The wait for the herald announcement turned into an obsession with news. As hope for the return started to fade with time, another was invented by the waiting refugees. The news obsession grew into an interest in politics at a newly expanded level. Cadres from the camps started to explore regional institutional change as the key to solving social and political injustice at the local level. Refugees concluded that their catastrophe (*Nakba*) was part of the larger Arab impediment in their struggle for unity, freedom and true independence. Hence, a number of Palestinian-inspired pan-Arab organizations were formed, such as the Pan-Arab Movement led by Dr George Habash, a recent Palestinian graduate of the American University at Beirut. This organization was the premier pan-Arab political party in the 1950s.

The social conditions in the camp created fertile ground for increased political awareness, even among those with only a rudimentary level of intellect. Circumstances in the camp and in the wider world inevitably promoted our interest at a very young age in political justice at both the emotional and intellectual levels. Like other children in the camp, I was a product of that same atmosphere where I became familiar with the Algerian struggle for independence, the struggle for equality in Africa, the US invasion of Vietnam and the civil rights movement in the United States. While Palestine was always the central focus in the development of my political consciousness, nevertheless I saw the struggle against injustice anywhere as complementary and congruent to the struggle for justice at home.

FIRST PUBLIC PROTEST

I was possibly six or seven years old when I participated in my first political demonstration. The protest was to oppose the visit of Tunisian president Bu-Ragibah to Lebanon in 1965 and his call a year earlier to accept a UN resolution dividing historical Palestine between Israelis and Palestinians. People in the camp felt betrayed, since Bu-Ragibah did not embrace a congruent call for the return of refugees to their original homes. I still have a clear recollection of the two main slogans from that demonstration. The first went: "Oh Bu-Ragibah you pig, you need to be tied with a chain." In Arabic, it had a much more synchronized lilting rhythm: *Ya Bu-Ragiba Ya Khanzeer, Bidak Rabit Bil Janzeer.* The second went: "Oh Bu-Ragibah, you are a brute, what brings you to Beirut", the rough Arabic translation with a masculine rhyming reverberation reading *Ya Bu-Ragibah Ya Akroot, Chu Jabak Ala Beirut.* About four years later, Nasser Askool, the young lead chanter and one of the demonstration's organizing committee, was killed in a shootout with the Lebanese police.

Askool was a member of the Pan-Arab Movement at the time.

The second mass rally I attended followed the defeat of the Arab armies in the 5 June war of 1967. Soon after the war was over, the Arab public realized that all historical Palestine was lost, along with the Sinai Desert from Egypt and the Golan Heights from Syria. Following the humiliating defeat, the president of Egypt, Gamal Abdul Nasser, announced his resignation on 9 June. Refusing to accept defeat, the Arab public filled the streets in impromptu mass demonstrations asking Nasser to rescind his resignation. I was among those millions as I joined the largest public gathering of its kind ever to take place in the camp. The organizers decided to march to the city of Tripoli to join yet another large protest in the second largest city in Lebanon. The distance from the camp to Tripoli was about four hours' walk. Halfway there, we received the news that Nasser had withdrawn his resignation. The demonstration was dispersed two hours away from home. My oldest brother was riding in a taxi when he saw me walking and asked the driver to pick me up in an already crammed car. It is fair to say that these two events in my early childhood were very instrumental in starting to shape my fledgling political consciousness.

On 21 March 1968, Palestinian guerrillas fought a relentless battle against an Israeli incursion into a town called Al Karamah at the border with Jordan. The guerrillas succeeded in pushing the Israeli army back in the first serious battle since the humiliating Arab defeat of 1967. The small armed guerrilla force received public affirmation and official approbation for standing up to Israel less than a year after the crushing defeat of three major Arab armies. At the time, the camp was still under the control of the Lebanese police and internal security forces. During the police reign, local political activists were frequently rounded up in the middle of the night and dragged for interrogation by the feared internal security. On 21 March 1969, the first anniversary of the Al Karamah battle, activists organized a large political event to commemorate the battle and to avow public support for the revolution. My oldest brother, Ghazi, was one of the main organizers at the event. At night, my dad was worried that the Lebanese security might "visit" our house as part of the roundup of activists following such events. We were instructed not to open the door to anyone without first looking through the side kitchen window. That night I discovered that Dad had an illegal 9 mm pistol at home. Having a handgun was unlawful and could land a person, especially a Palestinian refugee, with a long-term jail sentence in Lebanon. That night, however, my father was determined not to let anyone take his oldest son away without a fight. He placed the cocked gun on the counter next to the window for possible confrontation. Fortunately, no one showed up. Nevertheless, looking back at that little episode, I did not understand the momentousness of the situation at the time. However, it undoubtedly formed a part of my subconscious political evolution.

JOINING THE REVOLUTION

It was usual to observe various youth groups carrying out informal physical training around the camp. The young kids wanted to be in good shape if and when the call came to join the revolution. A group of us used to gather after school in an open field next to the river to perform physical fitness exercises. We trained in hand combat techniques and the famous back-flip from persons who had received semi-formal guerrilla training. Even though the ground was grassy and soft, at times we used to fall hard on our back yet act tough and indifferent to pain. After all, we called ourselves *Ashball Al Thawra*, or the "Cubs of the Revolution".

In summer 1969, we were ready to take the big step. Five of us started to plot a scheme to run away to Syria to join the revolution's military training camp. I was the youngest of the group at eleven years old. The leader of the plot, nicknamed "Churchill", was about three years older and the others were twelve and thirteen years of age. Churchill, who had run away earlier, claimed to be already a member of the revolution and to know where to go and how best to join the training base. The group included my longtime friend Mohamed, who is now the money exchange person in the camp, a neighbor's kid, and another schoolmate. Together we contrived a clandestine plot to raise funds to cover the travel cost to the Al Asifah (the Storm) training base near Damascus. Al Asifah, the military wing of Fatah, was the largest guerrilla organization, and Churchill claimed that he was a fully pledged member. We collected and sold brass scrap and bones, and dug sand from the beach. One member of the group sold a broken watch and another stole 5 Lebanese pounds from home. It took us about three weeks to raise enough money for one-way travel with a little extra for food. On the morning of D-day, Churchill collected the money, ordered us not to carry anything and to walk separately to a meeting location just outside the camp. The plan was to meet at a previously agreed spot to avoid suspicion or to be noticed by anyone who might alert our parents or the Lebanese police. The plan worked perfectly. We shared a taxi to the Lebanese–Syrian border crossing at the town of Dabusia. The driver dropped us a few meters from the Lebanese customs crossing office. Once outside the car, we walked unnoticed across the border checkpoint. The area was crowded with kids our age and carts selling goods to travelers. The border police must have confused us with the other kids or possibly never expected us to illegally cross the border. We walked past the Lebanese border inspection point for about a mile before reaching the Syrian side. A river known as the Big River marked the official border demarcation between Lebanon and Syria. We arrived at a Lebanese farm along the river when we were spotted by another boy from the camp. The boy, who was our age, worked as a laborer in a citrus grove on the Lebanese side of the border. He enquired about our intentions. After telling him our plans, we asked if he could suggest a good location to cross into Syria. He pointed us to a shallow crossing that would take us past the first Syrian border police station. We asked him to keep our mission secret and bade the boy goodbye.

To avoid the attention of the Syrian or Lebanese border officers, we decided to cross the river one by one. It was summer, and the river ran pretty shallow during that period. Once on the other side we were in Syria, the first time I had ever set foot in another country. Actually, it was also the first time I had left or planned to sleep outside my own home. Again, we walked innocuously past the various security checkpoints. We were not asked for our identifications and smoothly disappeared past all the checkpoints at the crowded borders. However, as we stood in the passengers' park looking for a car to take us to the closest town, a person gave us the scare of the day. He suddenly grabbed two of us and in a loud voice ordered us to stop and claimed to be from the Syrian secret service. Seconds later, he laughed and said he was jesting. He nevertheless scared me half to death. We waited in a small passenger van until it got full before traveling to the next Syrian town named Tal Klakh. In Tal Klakh we went to the main bus station and bought tickets to go to the city of Homs. At the main bus station in Homs, we took the bus to Damascus where we arrived in the late afternoon of a long summer day. At the main bus station, we took another small bus to a well-known Al Asifah base called Al Hammah, just outside Damascus. Al Hammah was well known because not long previously it had been bombarded by Israel. The bus dropped us off just before sunset on the main road outside the military camp. Churchill led us up the hill and made contact with the guard. He told him that we had arrived to join the revolution. The guard chuckled at first as he was taken aback by our young age. He asked us to wait outside and took Churchill to meet the base commander. The guard told the commander about the four children outside and informed him that Churchill was responsible for the recruitment. At first, Churchill greeted the base commander and expected recognition for his "patriotic" act. But the base commander was livid at him for coming back and now for bringing along four other children. We were called in and at that moment we realized that Churchill had been refused permission to join the *fedayeen* earlier, and had been told not to come back before he was at least sixteen years old! (The word *fedayeen* literally means those who are ready to sacrifice themselves for their cause.) The base commander was so annoyed he decided that Churchill should be physically disciplined before sending him back again. He was then taken to another room and was flogged with a hard stick on the soles of his feet until he started to scream. The commander was nicer to us, as we were spanked once on our back and told to return to school.

It was just after sunset when we were booted out of the base. We walked down the hill to the main road for another bus ride back to Damascus. At that point, we had enough money only for the short trip, but no place to go. As we waited and darkness loomed over our heads, our situation hit me hard, for it was my first night ever away from home and we had no place to stay. Riding on the bus to Damascus,

I sat quietly and kept looking through the window to see the reflection on the glass of a frightened and hungry child who was not sure where the night was going to take him. I wished the ride was longer, but all too soon the bus dropped us at the main station. We followed Churchill blindly like little chicks trailing the mother duck while hoping the elder duck knows her way. We walked for a bit and asked him if he knew where he was going. He did not; it was like the blind leading the blind. We walked past a mosque where someone suggested that we should go inside and find a place to sleep. The late evening prayer was just wrapping up when we entered the place. The mosque's custodian was getting ready to turn off the lights and lock up when he noticed five children remaining inside. He told us that prayer time was over and asked nicely for us to leave. Churchill told him that we had nowhere to go and needed a place to stay for the night. When the custodian found out why we were stranded, he started preaching to us about the importance of becoming religiously observant if we planned to join the revolution. After the talk, Churchill went to the water fountain for ablution before praying. The custodian felt sorry and allowed us to sleep outside the mosque in an enclosed area in the yard by the main door. The concrete floor was covered with straw mats. I was exhausted and ready to sleep anywhere. I rested my head on my right hand, taking the hard floor as my mattress and the stars in the dark sky as my cover sheet for the night. Even though it was warm during the day, we all had to coil up during the cool breeze of the early morning. Generally, just before 4 a.m., the mosque calls for the morning prayer over the loudspeakers. The pious must have walked around us or stepped over us to reach the praying hall, for I had no memory of hearing the call or waking up when the devout entered the place.

STREET BEGGAR

We were awoken later by the bright Damascus morning sun, hungry, confused and not knowing what to do next. We didn't have any money to buy food or for the long ride home. We discussed our options and considered working for food and a place to sleep. But we were too young for anyone to offer us a job, besides we were in Damascus illegally. Considering the limited choices, we opted to seek hand-outs from passers-by. At that very moment, I wished I didn't have hands to extend or beg for money. It was so degrading an option that I couldn't do it. I am still traumatized even today thinking about it. I sat on the outside wall of the mosque watching Churchill standing in the middle of the sidewalk, begging for change. Sitting by the wall, I was mortified and cried profusely, which inadvertently made walkers-by feel more sympathetic. Passers-by were generous and within half an hour we collected about one and a half Syrians pounds, a good sum of money in those days. Then, after giving us money, one individual wondered why we were begging on the street. Churchill explained that we were stranded with no money to go back to Lebanon after being turned away from joining the revolution.

I'm not sure if I believe in miracles, but that person was as close to a miracle as could have been. We could have been anywhere in the city, but it just so happened that we were about three blocks from a Fatah civilian office. Fatah was the organization we had attempted to join a day earlier. The man then suggested that we go to the office to explain our quandary. He pointed us the way and continued his walk. That was the best chance out of our humiliation. We walked in that direction, and after a while we stopped and asked a person selling cactus fruit on a cart about the Fatah office. He pointed to his customer who came from the same building.

We followed that individual and at the office we requested to see the person in charge. The person behind a metal desk looked at us as we stood by the door and asked if he could be of any help. We started to cry, all of us this time, and told him of our problem. Before even finishing, he called another person from the next room and told him to give each of us five Syrian pounds for food and the bus ride home. They must have dealt with this type of situation before, as the officer asked us to sign a cash receipt before taking us to the bus station.

We took the same trip in reverse, but made a mistake and asked the driver to drop us several miles from the Lebanese border. Churchill thought we were close to the border and wanted to elude the border police by crossing the border away from the checkpoint. We walked for hours and as the sun was setting, we realized that we were far from the border. We attempted to hitchhike with passing trucks but were not successful. By the time we arrived at the border, it was already very dark. We decided to just walk across the bridge as we didn't see any border police. On the Lebanese side, it was the same story, the post was almost deserted with no cars around. We were less than twenty miles from the camp. Since there were no cars, we were stranded once more, but at least this time we were already inside Lebanon.

There was a small Lebanese village next to the border checkpoint. We walked to the first house and asked for help. An older woman directed us to the village head or *mukhtar* up the hill. We knocked at the *mukhtar*'s modest house, and explained our problem to the lady answering the door. She quietly asked us to come inside. The woman knew that her family could face trouble for providing us with shelter, for we were "criminals" under Lebanese laws for crossing the border illegally and for attempting to join a military organization.

Despite all that, she must have felt pity toward us and decided to help. The *mukhtar* welcomed us and without asking if we were hungry, he asked his wife to prepare dinner for us. The *mukhtar* asked about our trip and was very happy that we were sent back: "You are too young to join the revolution, you can contribute more to your cause by finishing your school first," he said. The wife, who was setting out dinner on the rug, occasionally stopped to hear the story between her trips from the room to the kitchen. In a very short time, a good-sized meal was awaiting for us on the floor. We could not wait any longer, when the *mukhtar* invited us to start eating. We ate as if we had not seen food for days. I for one was tired of eating falafel sandwiches and was ready for a proper meal. While we ate, the wife was busy again, placing mattresses on the floor next to the living room. We washed up after dinner and went to sleep on fresh-smelling mattresses. We woke up early in the morning, thanked the *mukhtar* and his family for their hospitality and off we went, looking for a car to take us back to the camp.

CROSSING FROM CHILDHOOD TO MANHOOD

The camp was still controlled by Lebanese security and we were afraid that, if discovered, we would be arrested for crossing the border to join the revolution. To avoid suspicion, I and another boy were dropped just outside the camp and the other three were dropped in a closer area. The two of us separated soon after, and I decided to walk along the coastline to reach our neighborhood. I was afraid my father would be angry at me for running away and was hesitant about going home. Eventually, I arrived at our neighborhood where the UNRWA clinic was located. The beach in the area was lined by a large manmade bulwark of concrete cubes to protect the health facility from heavy winter sea storms. While I was trying to find my way between the concrete cubes, by sheer coincidence my father was standing by the door looking toward the beach when he noticed his runaway child. He smiled and ordered me to come over. He gave me a kiss and with a sense of pride he introduced me to an older gentleman as the "son who ran away to join the revolution". He then held my hand and started to walk me home. He never asked where I had been, or what I had done. He was just relieved it was over. My father rarely expressed his feelings verbally. He just never did; but I could sense his pride as we walked the five hundred feet toward our home. In addition to being glad that I was back, he was content with his young son who wanted to join the revolution. I found out later that he had been bragging about his eleven-year-old who went to Syria to become a rebel. Certainly he was pleased that I was rebuffed for being too young, but was proud nevertheless of the fact that I ran away for a good cause and not as a mischievous kid.

At home of course my mother had the biggest smile on her face, not just because I was back, but, like my dad she was ecstatic that I had not been allowed to join the revolution. I must say, I walked home as a different person. In only three days I must have crossed the line from childhood to manhood. At least that's how I felt. In the aftermath, I was pleased for not being admonished or made to feel guilty, unlike our neighbor's kid who was physically disciplined and was grounded. As soon as my mom got me to change out of my smelly clothes, I couldn't wait to go outside to join with other children in our neighborhood, to play and talk about my revolutionary adventure. My oldest brother sent little brother after me and asked me to come home. But like a new young man, I sent back my little brother with a message that I was busy and I would come home once I was done playing.

That must have been the new young man's first official act of defiance toward the oldest brother's authority.

THE REVOLUTION

The twenty-eighth of August 1969 was a nice, warm sunny day. I was fishing and searching for crabs along the shore near the river. The Friday before, I had sold a load of scrap animal bones and taken a ride to the neighboring Lebanese village to buy fishing material. Close by, I watched an individual using explosives to fish. The person tossed a dynamite stick at a school of fish and, as usual, I was getting ready to take off my clothes to help collect the dead fish. At the same time and out of nowhere, an out-of-breath friend came running to tell us about a large impromptu protest against the Lebanese police. He told us that the protesters had taken over the police station and were barricading the international road connecting Lebanon with Syria. I quickly put on my plastic sandals and along with the other kids ran alongside the river toward the main road. The camp's cemetery was located next to the river and we had to go through it to reach the police station. By the time we arrived at the cemetery, we saw an older masked man entrenched behind a tombstone with a gun pointed toward Lebanese security positions at the main bridge. I recognized the person as Abu Al Amin, also known as Mousa Al Zubaidi, a good friend of my father's. Mousa was killed several years later during the Lebanese Civil War. I suggested to my friends that we stay close by in a ditch and wait for the shooting to start so we could clap and give moral support to Mousa. We decided to sit in the channel and wait for the shooting to start. After five minutes or so, one friend became restless and wanted to go to the "center of action" at the police station. Mousa also did not want us to stay around and asked us to leave. We decided to move on and go to the police building.

As we arrived, we realized that the protest had been provoked by the police arrest of a person named Abu Atif, the father of Atif, also known as Ahmed Cha'baan. Ahmed had allegedly been building a room in his backyard to operate as an office for the Fatah organization, the main rebel group in the PLO. Months earlier, Atif, Ahmed's eldest son, had run away to Syria to join the revolution. Atif was receiving training at the same base where we had tried to join the rebel group several months earlier. Ahmed decided to go after his son and bring him home. He arrived at the base and demanded his son return home. The base commander, who had sent us back with a spank earlier, told Ahmed that his son was old enough to decide for himself, but he would have no choice but to send Atif back if he insisted. Ahmed demanded to see his son. The base commander was obliged and called Atif in for the meeting. Atif walked into the room dressed in green fatigue, kissed his dad's hand and sat next to him with an AK47 on his lap. The son and father were left alone for their reunion and some privacy. I came to know years later that Ahmed had mixed feelings of intimidation and pride as he watched his eldest son seated next to him as an equal. Ahmed told Atif of his mother's grief and how much she would like him to come back home. Fighting back his tears, Atif said how much he missed his mother and little brother. But now he had a new mother and many more little brothers in the revolution. Atif pleaded with his dad to allow him to finish his military training and to join the revolution. His father was moved by how much Atif had grown and by his transformation in the short time since he had joined the training camp. Abruptly, Ahmed stood up and called the base commander back into the room. The base commander, who was about six feet tall, with an athletic figure and receding hair, walked into the room in anticipation of Ahmed's final decision. Ahmed walked toward the base commander, extended his arm to shake his hand and to the surprise of both Atif and the base commander, Ahmed said: "I want to stay here too. I want to join the revolution." The base commander was pleased to welcome Ahmed as the newest member of Fatah's military wing, Al Asifah or "The Storm".

After receiving his basic training, Ahmed slipped back into the camp and was charged with the task of opening a conscription office for Fatah, the political wing of Al Asifah. Since space was limited in the camp, Ahmed decided to build an extra room in his backyard to become the new organization's office. A security informant must have alerted the authority of the illegal construction. The Lebanese security arrived at the scene, issued a citation, and ordered Ahmed to cease all building activities. After refusing the enforcement order, Ahmed was detained and dragged into the police station. The security force transferred him immediately to a regional detention center outside the camp for further interrogation.

The news of Ahmed's arrest spread like wildfire throughout the camp. Following his detention, residents started to gather and establish a human barrier around the construction site. Soon thereafter an impromptu demonstration ensued with a march toward the police station, demanding the release of the detainee. The local police commander told the demonstrators that Ahmed had been transferred for questioning at the regional headquarters. The police couldn't contain the protesters as their numbers swelled up to thousands in no time. The local police chief was caught by surprise, and before he could call for additional reinforcement to help defend the police station, the citizens' rage turned into a maelstrom as the fuming demonstrators assaulted the police station, breaking windows and throwing the office furnishing onto the main road. The local police commander ordered the security force to evacuate the station.

A young person, who was familiar with the layout of the police station, led a group of young men to the weaponry storage room and seized the police rifles and hand guns. A large truckload of military reinforcements soon arrived outside the police station. The intrepid crowd attacked the truck with sticks and rocks. The military contingent left the truck and ran away toward the bridge just outside the camp. The crowd dragged the truck into the middle of the highway bisecting the camp, flipped the truck over and set it ablaze. The road was at the time the only access route connecting the Lebanese areas north of the camp to other parts of Lebanon. The road was also the lifeline artery connecting Lebanon with Syria. At the same time, the regional area commander of the Lebanese security ordered the immediate release of the prisoner. Ahmed, who had not been well known before the protest, had become a virtual hero. His release though was too little too late, as the rolling snowball turned into a public avalanche of anger and rage.

The police station was ransacked and the young men who seized the police handguns and rifles took fighting positions across from the main bridge. When we arrived at the station, it was almost clear but for flying papers and a huge mess on the floor. I took a short tour of the chief of police's office and the small jail cell next door, recalling the names and faces of the many people who had either spent time there or were flogged on the old wooden chair. For the first time in my life, I was inside the police station where I traded my classic trepidation with jubilation. I was ecstatic to be inside the same structure that used to instill fear in me just by looking at it or even passing it by on the road. The building was the center of intimidation, humiliation and horror in the camp. For the first time, I felt that the camp was finally free and in complete control of its destiny.

Meanwhile, people were still gathering and the crowd grew larger and larger. I saw individuals carrying hunting guns, a person with a hand grenade, another with a handgun, and only one person with an automatic machine gun. The blaze from the burning truck was getting higher as the demonstrators started to throw the furnishings from the police station over the burning vehicle. I will never forget the horn sounding from the burning truck and how abruptly it was silenced. We continued to jump and chant around the blaze-engulfed truck when suddenly and without any warning the shooting erupted. We ran for cover into the alleys. The Lebanese security, with additional military reinforcement, had decided to retake the police station and enter the camp by force.

The lightly armed fighters fought back with amazing resolve. The Lebanese security and an army contingent led by a light armored vehicle attempted to cross the bridge. I saw a Lebanese soldier standing behind the heavy machine gun on the top of the armored vehicle, shooting indiscriminately toward the gathering crowd. You could hear clearly the sound of bullets buzzing overhead and ricocheting from nearby structures, when unexpectedly the heavy machine gun ceased shooting simultaneously with a strong squeal as the army gunner tumbled from the armored vehicle to drop into the river five meters below. Surprised by the tough resistance, the Lebanese security forces pulled back from the bridge and took combat positions across on the other shore. The shooting continued for several hours before an informal ceasefire was agreed to in the early evening. In an amazing grace, the camp's residents or fighters had suffered no fatal injuries. The fighters were very pleased with the break in fighting. One of the fighters (*fedayeen*) confided to me that the camp defenders were almost out of ammunition and were no match for the Lebanese army. I suspect the Lebanese army also did not have the will to fight, as many of them sympathized with the Palestinian revolution and the *fedayeen* cause. It also became known later that the prime minister of Lebanon objected to the use of force to enter the camp. Soon after the informal ceasefire, camp elders started to negotiate with the Lebanese security forces to ease the siege and to reopen the main highway connecting Lebanon with Syria. The Lebanese security forces took positions over the hills and installed military checkpoints inspecting all vehicles entering or leaving the camp. At the same time, the army continued to demand the unconditional surrender of the fighters.

Soon thereafter, other Palestinian camps in Lebanon revolted and evicted the police. Other more serious confrontations ensued between the Palestinian *fedayeen* and the Lebanese army in other parts of Lebanon, mainly in the south. Mediation between Lebanon and the Palestine Liberation Organization (PLO) succeeded in reaching an agreement to regulate the relationship between the newly armed Palestinian guerilla fighters and the Lebanese army. Under the auspices of Gamal Abdul Nasser, president of Egypt, Yasser Arafat and the Lebanese president, Charles Hilu, signed in November 1969 what became known as the Cairo Accord. As part of the ceasefire agreement, the Lebanese government agreed to cede control of Palestinian camps and to provide the PLO with the freedom to operate in south Lebanon.

Life in the camp changed significantly after the Palestinian revolution's entry. Armed and political Palestinian organizations established several offices throughout the camp, and for the first time started to recruit openly for new members. At least seven organizations set up political offices, three of them in our neighborhood alone. The new groups were not just military or political organizations. They also established clinics, social services and youth centers. Ideologically speaking, they were a mixture of pan-Arab groups, internationalist, secular and nationalist organizations. Considering the elevated level of sectarian politics today, none of the rebel organizations at that time had any direct religious affiliation or sectarian propensity; to the contrary, at least two were inclined towards Marxism. In the absence of Lebanese law enforcement, the new organizations established among themselves a coordinating committee to monitor security and order. Two years after this new-found freedom, the camp became a beehive of construction activities as people started to expand their homes and replace the tin sheeting with concrete roofs. During the Lebanese security era, construction was severely restricted in the camp; people couldn't even get a permit to replace dilapidated tin sheeting with new concrete roofing. Multiple families used to share the same quarters in cramped rooms. Following the evacuation of the Lebanese security forces, permits were not required for new room expansions or to replace tin sheeting with concrete.

Considering the limited space and growing families, home expansion usually meant building second story units. With the lack of planning and space limitation, the camp became a huge cinder-block sprawl. None of the new dual story concrete structures were engineered properly. The greenery, mostly grape vines in homes, was replaced by concrete edifices. The small alleys became even narrower as residents encroached on public pathways. And where alleys were already too small to be infringed upon, people started to extend their concrete roofs. In fact, prior to its destruction in the summer of 2007, a person could walk in many areas inside the camp without seeing the sun or getting wet during rain.

SMUGGLING WEAPONS FOR THE PLO

My father continued to work with UNRWA as an ambulance driver to transport medical referrals three times a week from the two Palestinian camps in north Lebanon to major hospitals in Beirut. He typically left home around four in the morning and came back after two in the afternoon. Often he took along illicit non-patients for a free ride in the ambulance to Beirut or beyond. For impecunious persons, it really meant a big saving on the weekly travel cost to work or to attend college in the capital.

Following their evacuation in 1969, the freed camps were placed under total siege by the Lebanese army. During this period, a student leader in one of the Palestinian organizations named Majed approached my dad about a large parcel he needed to deliver to one of the Palestinian camps in Beirut. Majed, who was a member of the political wing of the PFLP, had been tasked with delivering the urgent parcel within two days. He contacted my dad and enquired about the next scheduled trip to Beirut's hospitals. "Tomorrow morning", he was told. Majed revealed only that the camps were in dire need of the package. While recognizing that the package could have contained prohibited materials, my dad never asked the student leader to disclose the items in the bag. My father trusted Majed enough and felt it was the least that could be done to help the besieged camps.

Just before 4.00 a.m., the young man was waiting outside our house ahead of the arriving elderly sick patients. Dad helped carry the heavy bag into the ambulance and suggested stowing it away in the compartment under the back seats. Soon thereafter, the rest of the travelers arrived and the ambulance departed the camp. At about 4.30 a.m., the ambulance advanced toward the military checkpoint on the outskirts of the camp. The guard requested identification papers and medical referrals for each of the passengers. After careful inspection, the soldier noticed no medical transfer document for the young individual sitting in the back of the ambulance. A soldier enquired about the young man's doctor referral, and when he could not provide one, they became suspicious and ordered all the passengers out of the ambulance. At first my dad attempted to convince the soldiers that the young man was an escort for one of the elderly sick women. The head soldier was adamant about searching the vehicle. Then my father raised it a notch, to protest the dislodging of sick elderly patients from the ambulance. He demanded to plead his case to the military commander. The plea request and incessant objections were ignored. Two officers climbed into the ambulance to search the cupboards under the back seats' cushions. The officers discovered a large package and enquired about the goods. My father was confounded, but Majed jumped to the front and told the soldiers that the package was his alone and no one else was aware of it. The soldiers inspected the large package and discovered a bag full of gun ammunition. The sick passengers were taken for further interrogation, while the young chap, my father and the ambulance were taken into custody. About two hours later we were awakened to the news of my father's arrest for smuggling illegal ammunition to the revolution in Beirut.

The news of my dad's arrest was overwhelming to us, and especially to my mother. I had very mixed feelings, sad but at the same time proud. Deep in my heart, I believed my dad was doing the right thing in trying to help the besieged camps. During all my childhood, my father was my role model and I always looked up to him for support. But now, I was heartbroken to see him in jail with hardened criminals. After the arrest, he was placed in the most feared prison in Lebanon, named Rumie; a jail famous for executing convicted murderers. Suddenly the family routine was disrupted by the absence of the family patriarch. At night, it was time to reckon with the new reality. He had always been a family man, and would usually be at home just before sunset to eat dinner and go to bed early for his 4 a.m. trip to Beirut. The arrest meant that we became even more frugal in our expenditure. The allowance was curtailed, food was rationed, and gloom replaced normalcy in our house.

While kids are always kids, nevertheless all of us had to be content with the adjustment and the little sacrifices when considering what our father was going through in jail. I will never forget the day my mother was allowed to visit him in prison, leaving her two-year-old daughter at home. Unusually for me, I volunteered to babysit my sister Aziza while my mother went to Beirut to call on Dad. It was important for Mom not to feel guilty about leaving us alone for the day; for as long as I remember, she had never been anywhere outside the camp for more than a couple of hours at the most. Taking care of Aziza was an act of solidarity with Mom and Dad during those tough times. I took my little sister along to the neighborhood playground where she sat to watch us older kids play. When she was ready for her afternoon nap, I put her on my lap and sat under the shade of a hedgerow bamboo farm fence on the side of the road. The small asphalted road was the only access for cars to enter our neighborhood. I sat while Aziza slept under the shade, hoping that my mother would show up at any minute to tell me about my dad. Many cars passed, but the vehicle bringing her never appeared. My mom did not come home until late in the day. I was anxious to hear about how Dad was holding out in prison. Arriving home, my mother was very sick and throwing up, as she had got motion sickness from the long car ride. The long trip, combined with seeing Dad on the other side of the prison bars, was very distressing. Watching her vomiting and the sad face left me torn up from inside out.

At nighttime, I used to think a lot about my father's life in jail. Many nights, I used to cry myself to sleep silently so my mother wouldn't notice, and to still act tough in front of my younger brothers and sister. I, too, was not able to handle the thought that my dad was in jail with street-hardened criminals. I didn't appreciate it at that time, but my father and mother were more worried about his job, our only source of income. If he was not released soon or if he was convicted in court, UNRWA would be obliged to terminate his employment. Driving an ambulance for UNRWA provided us with a decent life in the camp and the thought of him losing his secured job was nerve-racking to my parents.

Fortunately, UNRWA employees in the local office in north Lebanon were all Palestinian refugees and the person in charge of all UNRWA local operations was a sympathizer with the rebel group accused of attempting to smuggle the ammunition. The first order of business for the local UNRWA staff was to provide a justification for the presence of the healthy passenger in the ambulance. Second was to submit reports to UNRWA headquarters in Beirut maintaining the driver's innocence. In 1969, there was widespread support for the revolutionary movement among both Palestinians and Lebanese. Many people wanted to help in any way possible. During the military interrogations, my father denied any knowledge of the smuggled ammunition in his car. Majed, the accused smuggler, supported my dad's contention and took complete responsibility for the ammunition. Several weeks later my dad was released on bond.

I was in school when a friend peeked into the classroom, announcing my father's release. While I was not able to leave the classroom, I did not learn much that afternoon, as I was physically at school but mentally at home with my free dad. Arriving home after a long day at school, I found a house packed with camp residents who had come to celebrate his freedom with the family. The community's joy was tempered though by the anticipation of a future court date to adjudicate on his guilt or innocence.

After a court date was set several months into the future, my dad was still worried that a conviction would mean certain job termination and loss of his pension. At the time, he could not afford a lawyer to defend him in court, and to make things worse, the court would not assign one for his defense either. Even though my dad was only a simple driver who could not read or write, he was exceptionally gifted at building relationships and was successful in establishing a strong network with high-level staff in UNRWA and the outside community. Those relations came in handy as he started to plead his case to anyone with potential political influence in Lebanon. He solicited help from the head of the PLO office in Beirut, Shafiq Al Hut, and from others who could potentially exert pressure on the court. The main help came from a person who had a strong association with the Syrian government. The person, named Fakhri, was originally from the camp, but lived in Beirut. It is important to note, however, that the most decisive support came from the passenger accused of smuggling the ammunition. Along with the testimony from the patients, Majed, who was a single person of about twenty-one years of age, took full responsibility for the ammunition and asserted to the court that the ambulance driver did not know about the bag. He was an honorable person who sacrificed himself so my dad could save his job and avoid a jail sentence. Since there was an admission of guilt, the judge found my dad not guilty and the young man was jailed for several years with hard labor.

The student leader was freed after serving most of his sentence at the infamous Rumie jail. Not long before these events, Majed had graduated from a two-year UNRWA-run technical institution. Subsequent to his release, he landed a job in the growing oil economies of the Gulf region and was able to leave the camp and his troubles behind.

4

Israeli Military Raids

— —

GUERILLA TRAINING

At the stage of life when I was getting ready to finish middle
school, I started to ponder on my future prospects as another
Palestinian refugee. Muslims are brought up to believe
that one's destiny is preordained well before birth. This
notwithstanding, the choices in life are still ours to make. In
other words, the final station is determined, but it is left
for humans to decide the journey or how best to reach that
destination.

At that age, I hoped to become a fighter pilot, but
how and where? Palestinians in Lebanon could not even
join the Lebanese army, far less become fighter pilots. After
the PLO took charge of the camps, other opportunities became
available for students with at least a high school diploma. The
PLO is an umbrella grouping of several independent political

and military organizations. Based on their sponsorship or ideological affiliation, each of the member organizations established special global relationships or alliances, mostly with revolutionary or communist governments. To promote themselves and as part of their recruiting strategies, they offered scholarships for students wishing to study engineering or medicine in many of the eastern bloc countries and as far away as Cuba. In some internal circles, there was discussion also about sending students to countries like Algeria, among other places, to train as fighter pilots. These possibilities offered me enough of a ray of hope that I was encouraged to continue my education and stay at school, instead of quitting to learn a trade skill early on in life, like the majority of my friends.

Meanwhile, the unit in charge of public security and police in the camp initiated a program to arm and provide basic military training to middle school pupils. Along with a number of other kids, I joined what became known as the "Patriot Unit". As the name inferred, the new unit had no political affiliation to any of the organizations. I was assigned a Siminoff rifle with ten bullets. The Siminoff was an old semi-automatic weapon with one 10-bullet magazine. It was a remnant of the Soviet WWII military industry. The rifle, which used the same bullets as the more renowned AK-47, was as tall as or even taller than I was at the time. The Patriot Unit was under the tutelage of a corporal in the security division, who was likely bored and looking for something to do when he recognized an opportunity to keep some of the teenagers busy after school. His acolyte, our trainer, was a younger man who did not come from the camp. The trainer had a necklace with a cross that sat on the middle of his chest. The cross got my attention as it was possibly the first time I had met a Christian in rebel fatigues. Frankly, the only

Christians I knew of until then were well-to-do Lebanese Christians who were either right-wingers or too snooty to wear green military uniform, far less sleep in a military mess hall. I befriended the training instructor and found out that he was a Palestinian from one of the Christian camps in Lebanon. The two Palestinian Christian camps were located in the midst of Lebanese Christian neighborhoods. Before the civil war, Lebanon had two Palestinian Christian camps. After the war, only one Christian camp survived while the other camp was razed by the right-wing militia of the so-called Lebanese Christian forces. The other Christian camp was saved at the last minute only after the Vatican's ambassador intervened directly with the head of the right-wing Phalangeist party, Pierre Gemayel. I was aware of Christians (mostly Lebanese) working in the camp and remember hearing my mother talking about the nice Christian nurses that worked at the UNRWA clinic during the early years in the camp, or the Lebanese Christian UNRWA doctor. However, I'd never known or dealt directly with any Christian at a personal level. My Christian trainer was tough, more so than the corporal. He made us run long distances and jump hard as part of the daily strenuous physical exercise. I showed him as much respect as any teenager could exhibit to a militaristic authority. Trudging to the training area, I was assigned to lead the column while carrying a heavy machine gun over my shoulder. It was a highly revered role heading the march in the middle of the camp, especially if the march would pass by the house of my girl at the time, which it did. I must confess that the task was demanding, carrying the heavy gun, setting the tone for the column's disposition, and still acting tough even when soaked in sweat under the heat of the sun.

My favorite of all the training activities, and one I still enjoy to this day, was target shooting. The unit could not afford target practice often, but during our three months' training we did so twice. I hit the target two out of three attempts in the first practice session. The second time around, I missed two and hit the target only once. After the second shooting practice, my dad asked at home how many I had hit. I felt embarrassed and feigned getting two shots out of three. Even then he said, "Why did you miss the third shot, you just need to hold the gun hard against your shoulder, keep your eye on the mark, hold your breath and fire. Try doing better next time."

ISRAELI SEA RAID

As part of the training, we also used to conduct a night watch outside the camp. For a fourteen-year-old teenager, it was more like spending a night out in a trench at the beach with other kids. We kept an eye toward the sea, drank hot tea all night long and poked fun at each other, especially if one of us snoozed while on duty. To punish a sleeping guard, we would hide the magazine from his rifle and have him beg to get it back. Like most of my friends, I never took guard duty very seriously. It never occurred to me that Israeli commandos might travel this far and so close to the Syrian border to conduct a sea raid on the camp in the middle of the night. Although Israeli military planes had raided the camp just a few months earlier, I still thought the chances of an Israeli sea raid were practically nil. But I was wrong.

About a week after one of our stints on night watch duty, around 1 a.m. one morning in February 1973, we were awakened to the sounds of explosions and heavy shooting. By now my father had begun to sleep in our bedroom, as my oldest brother Ghazi had got married and taken over the other room he had previously shared with my dad. I slept on a military- or clinic-like bed with chains supporting a sponge mattress on one side of the room. Between my bed and my dad's was a small table with an old radio that used to wake us up every morning at 6 a.m. to the news program from the BBC Arabic station. On the other side of the room was my older brother Majed, sleeping on anther old bed. Five other family members slept on the floor between the two beds: my mother, sister and three younger brothers. When my father asked about the shooting, my older brother said something to the effect that it must have been night training for the *fedayeen*. It was not unprecedented, albeit not very common, for us to be awakened to the sound of bullets at night. The shooting this time, however, was too close to our house, was heavy and the explosions were louder. Then suddenly we started to hear public commotions outside our house, as people realized the camp was being attacked by an Israeli commando force.

The Israeli raid targeted a community clinic for the Popular Front for the Liberation of Palestine (PFLP) in our neighborhood. The small building was empty but for the lonely unarmed night security guard who was sleeping inside. The guard had a dual job function. He worked as a pharmacy technician during the day and a night watchman after hours. The small building was completely demolished and the guard was killed on the spot. In the middle of the night, women carried their children and left our neighborhood seeking safer areas toward the center of the camp. Israeli military helicopters hovered low over our neighborhood. The piercing buzzing reverberation from the flying copters was deafening and scary. I saw our long-time neighbor Omar for the last time that night. He was carrying an AK-47 just outside our house. The targeted clinic was located three houses down a small alley from our home. Omar decided to go down the alley to defend the neighborhood, but that was a big mistake. The semi-straight alley was a death trap as the Israelis positioned sharpshooters at the entrance of the alley to shoot at anyone spotted in the area. Not realizing this, Omar didn't stand a chance: halfway from our house, he was shot dead. I heard his last shriek as he fell down. Under heavy gun fire, my uncle crawled down the alley to pull Omar back. It was already too late, as Omar's body was riddled with bullets. At the same time, my father attempted to take his machine gun up onto the roof to shoot at the attacking Israelis. Neighbors pleaded with him not to shoot from the house so as not to give the Israelis an excuse to destroy our neighborhood. It was, and still is, very common for Israelis to shell civilian neighborhoods indiscriminately and disproportionally under the specious pretext of self-defense. Meanwhile, I took out my Seminoff rifle and stood guard by the outside door, pacing the area from our house to the home where my mother and little brothers and sister were taking shelter. Then, and suddenly for a short ten minutes, the shooting exchange intensified between the Israelis in our neighborhood and the area at the north end of the camp. We learned later that the Israeli commandos had landed small boats at two locations to attack the PFLP clinic in our neighborhood and at the north end of the camp to attack the community police unit. Their plan seemed to have been that once they accomplished their mission in destroying the PFLP clinic and the police unit, the two commando units would meet in an open area next to the school yard to be lifted out by the hovering helicopters. Not knowing about the second Israeli commando group, we assumed that the ensuing shooting was between the Israeli commando group and the camp's police. We discovered later that the shooting was actually between the two Israeli companies. While the Israeli commandos from the south were retreating toward the site of the landing and possibly out of a combination of fear and confusion, the two Israeli commando units got into a cross fire among themselves before realizing their deadly mistake.

In the meantime, a group of the camp defenders, including my father and his nephew Salah, got together to attack the retreating Israeli commandos by the school. The group, armed with light machine guns and one grenade launcher called an RPJ7 moved toward the area where the copters were to land. As one copter started to hover low over the presumed landing site, the fighter with the RPJ7, under heavy gunfire cover from my dad and his company, dashed into the open and in a hurry aimed the grenade launcher at the landing helicopter. The pilot must have spotted the fighter and made a fast maneuver whereby the RPJ7 barely missed its target. The copter took off again and started along with the waiting Israeli boats at sea and soldiers on the ground to shoot aimlessly at the camp's defenders. The Israeli commandos retreated to another area behind a small building and were airlifted by the copters before sunrise. The RPJ7 was notorious for its imprecision, as it was another WWII military Soviet invention designed to shoot slow-moving objects such as tanks and from very short distances.

As the first sunlight of the day cleared the smoke, we saw the extent of the Israeli devastation from the previous night. In addition to those murdered, the Israelis left behind the ruins of the clinic, a devastated UNRWA ration distribution center and the flattened building of the police unit. Standing by the UNRWA food ration center, I distinctively remember how one slashed-open flour sack got the attention of two foreign newspaper correspondents. The journalists were taking pictures of the demolished UN ration center when they noticed the USAID emblem on the flour sack with an imprint of two shaking hands under the sketch of a US flag with the words "From the American People". The two journalists started to take pictures of the flour sacks, and from what I was able to understand, one of them was saying how ironic it was that the sack of flour had been donated by the US to help the hungry, only to be ruined by US-made weapons supplied to Israel.

The three demolished sites became a center of attraction for visitors and spectators who came from neighboring Lebanese towns and other places as a show of solidarity with the camp and to observe first-hand the level of Israeli destruction. In the afternoon I was hanging around the destroyed clinic in our neighborhood when I saw two speeding incoming jeeps. The jeeps made an abrupt turn and stopped by the clinic. A retinue surrounded a short man with a *kufiah* (head cover) who jumped out of one of the vehicles to inspect the rubble. We immediately recognized the person as the PLO leader Yasser Arafat, or Abu Ammar as he was commonly known among Palestinians. It was the first public visit by Arafat to the camp. Along with the other children, I ran toward Arafat to shake his hand. He was an energetic and very gracious individual. Like always, news spread fast in the camp and people rushed to meet their leader. The spontaneous gathering started to chant, "We sacrifice our blood and soul for Abu Ammar." Arafat admonished us and said no, for our chant should be, "We sacrifice our blood and soul for Palestine." In November 2004, when Arafat passed away, I wrote an article under the heading "Arafat, the Leader I Knew", which was published by the *San Diego Union Tribune* describing my first encounter with Yasser Arafat thirty years before his death.

SURVIVING THE FIRST ISRAELI AIR RAID

In the summer of 1972, a city girl was spending the summer with her relatives two houses down from our home. She was an average-looking girl but wore more up-to-date designer clothing, meaning that her dress was less conservative than that of the average girl in the camp. She immediately got my attention as well as the interest of many other boys in our neighborhood. It didn't help that she was a real flirt. In addition to the alley behind our house, we met in a nice green area by the river in the afternoons. Similar to my previous love crush experience in the camp, the word "meeting" might be an overstatement, for it was more like being in the same general area. My female cousin, who befriended the city girl, was our intermediary. Early in the day, my cousin told me that the girls planned to go to the river around 5 p.m. I asked a good friend of mine to join me to play in the area and to hang around the girls. The field was located less than a quarter of a mile from our house at the southern edge of the camp. We left our neighborhood around 4.40 p.m., and about halfway, we passed by a bike rental shop. Based on the amount of money paid, the bikes were usually rented by the hour, or even for just a few minutes, or for a ride from the store to a certain distance and back. I had 10 Lebanese pennies to spare and decided to take a bike ride to the cemetery and back. The cemetery was located at the edge of the camp next to the river, some 1,000 feet away. My friend waited in the shade as I propelled the bike for the short ride. It was early September 1972, around 4.45 p.m. By the time I arrived at the cemetery, I heard a jet-humming overhead. There was a Lebanese military airport just about twelve miles north of the camp, where military jets used to carry out flying exercise missions weekdays in the morning, but almost never in the afternoon. So it was odd to hear fighter jets at that time of the day. I slowed down the bike, attempting to look over my right shoulder toward the heavens above when I saw the biggest explosion I had ever seen in my life. It was a huge burst of flames covering a vast area around the field where we were supposed to be meeting with the girls a short time later. The first detonation was followed by a series of explosions throughout the open area on the other side of the river. The river and part of the cemetery were the dividing line between the bombing and my location. Immediately, I turned the bike around and sped back to the bike shop. I was panicking so badly that I didn't pedal the bike back. I just pulled it next to me while running for safety. The road was bounded by an irrigation channel to the left and a drainage channel on the other side. I vividly remember water spattering from falling debris and shrapnel. At the time, though, I suspected, albeit mistakenly, that I was being strafed from the air with the pilot missing me as the supposed bullets hit the water in the nearby drainage channel. During those perilous moments, I experienced a strange psychological transformation by which I transcended the stage of fear. Then and there I had no recollection of being frightened. I was just busy dodging the flying bullets fired by the pilots, or so I thought (I suppose watching war movies can make one delusional at times.) My first concern was to defeat the pilots by running zigzag on the road. The very short distance back to the bike shop was possibly the longest I've ever had to run for my life. About twenty feet from the shop, I gave up on pulling the bike. I dropped it, ran into the shop and told the owner that the bike was outside. The terrified shop owner who was taking cover inside couldn't care less where the bike was. He asked me to take shelter with him, but I decided to sprint through the shop's back door to disappear into the small alleys. The camp then did not have any anti-aircraft defenses, and not one single shot was fired back at the attacking planes. Unchecked, the sonorous American-made Israeli fighter jets continued their assaults by flying additional sorties over the defenseless camp. They repeatedly fired their missiles into the open field while I kept on navigating my way through the intricate alleys toward our house. By that time all my brothers and sister were already inside the home. The alleys in the camp were completely deserted, but for my mom who was still standing outside the door waiting for her impish offspring, and boy was she relieved to see him running home. She pulled hard on my hand and ordered me to get inside at once. I told her the raid was over and that the planes were gone by now. She fired back, "You're so naive. You don't know these people. They took our homes in Palestine, and now they want us defeated in our refugee camp." She closed the door behind me and said, "In 1948, and each time following their pernicious attacks, the Zionist terror organizations used to pretend to be gone before suddenly re-emerging again to carry on with their malignant, fiendish attacks. That was their way of telling us that going back to our homes meant certain death."

The planes did not come back that day. Nevertheless, my mother was proven right about the "certain death". For one of the Israeli tactics this time around was to drop several missiles equipped with timed delay devices to blow up in the aftermath of the raid. This policy intended to kill and maim as many people as possible, either directly or by creating an atmosphere of panic to delay medical assistance for the injured, hence increasing the number of fatalities. That was exactly what happened to the many civilians and paramedics who came to help the injured or to remove the dead. Several hours following the initial air raid, we continued to hear loud blasts where almost as many civilians were killed by the missiles with timed delay devices as those who had been killed during the primary raid.

After the raid, my mother allowed me to stand by the outside door where I held the Seminoff rifle on my shoulder, watching people walk by our house. And there was the city girl carrying her suitcase and leaving the camp in a hurry. At first, I was relieved that the girls were safe, as they too had been on their way to the river at the time of the Israeli raid. The fleeing girl smiled at me one last time as she left for good. She never came back to visit her relatives again in the camp. I didn't think much of it at the time, but looking back, the city girl had other options to consider. Meanwhile, the rest of us, the "people of the camp", had no choice but to submit to our inexorable fate.

Other mothers and fathers were not as lucky, as they waited in vain for the return of their loved ones after the attack. The air raid took place just before sunset, when the area was full of kids and families enjoying an outing after a warm summer day. Families used to go to lie on the green grass and enjoy the cool sea breeze. Kids swam in the river or the sea, and teenage boys hung around girls. Many of my friends and neighbors were killed on that dreadful summer day. One friend, Barakat, was also a member of my training unit. I used to tease him during our marches and while jogging during training. His dad raised milking goats and it was Barakat's chore to take the goats to the river green for grazing. Barakat had been in the middle of the field when the air raid started. He had no chance in the face of those huge missiles, and neither did his goats. Another neighbor, a six-year-old child named Mehdi Khalil, the brother of a friend of mine, was playing in the field during the raid. His body was never even retrieved. He was either blown to smithereens by a direct hit or was buried under the huge mounds of dirt left behind in the field.

Had the air raid started fifteen minutes later, my friends and I would have been in the middle of the field too. In fact, I was twice lucky that day: that same morning, our training unit had conducted one of our target practices in the same field. Indeed, that had been the last time I gave Barakat a hard time about missing his mark. He had looked at me with his usual diffident smile and said: "Let's wait and find out your score, smarty." And find out he did, as that was the time when I only managed one hit out of three. Another member of our unit was also killed in the air raid. He was a much older man, the only older person in the unit, as the rest were school-age youths. He worked as a fruit picker on the neighboring Lebanese farms and couldn't make it to the target practice in the morning. He must have been either confused about the time or had decided to carry out the target practice alone later that day. When he got home from work in the late afternoon, he had picked up his Seminoff rifle and gone to the target shooting area by the river. He was found dead just meters away from my location when the bombing started.

September 1972 must bring memories to many people. The opening ceremonies of the Olympic Games were in full swing in Munich, Germany. The Palestinian Black September group entered the Olympic village and took members of the Israeli team hostage. The group was demanding the release of Palestinian prisoners in Israeli jails in exchange for the safe release of the Israeli team. At first it appeared Israel and Germany would agree to free the Palestinian prisoners to secure the release of the Israeli sports team. In reality, Israel and the German authorities were setting a trap for the Black September group at the airport, where the exchange between Israel and the Palestinians was to take place. In a botched military operation, Israeli commandos attacked the Palestinian group in an attempt to free the Israeli hostages. At the end, most members of the Israeli team, as well as members of Black September, were killed. Supposedly, Israel raided my camp in retaliation for the Black September attack in Munich, even though Black September had no presence in the camp. The fate of the Israeli team at the Munich Olympics is recorded in history, with a Hollywood movie and many books written about it. However, it is certain that not many have heard of the innocent children killed by Israeli planes in Nahr-el-Bared Camp that same month.

One may, of course, understand an act of retaliation that is directly or indirectly associated with those who are accused of carrying out certain acts. But in September 1972, the families who were enjoying their summer outing, the kids who were swimming, or indeed the grazing goats, all had nothing to do with Black September. But to justify the killing of innocent civilians, Israel called its raid "retaliation", when in fact it was an act of vengeance intended to cause the most damage to another civilian target.

The irony was that during the Second World War, the Nazis carried out similar "retaliations" in places like France, Czechoslovakia and Greece. When a German soldier was killed by the Resistance, they would massacre an entire village, whose residents, albeit sympathetic, had little to do with the rebels. This kind of Nazi reprisal was quite rightly considered to be a war crime.

Israel stands out among nations in its invention of linguistic sophistry to justify acts of retribution. Israel exploited the written and spoken language by substituting the words "retaliation" for "revenge", "pre-emptive" for "aggression", and "defense" to justify war. Among them all, the mother of all contorted Israeli lexicons was the word "pre-emptive", as Israel defined its 1967 war. Israel claimed and continues to claim that it had to preempt an attack by three Arab countries: Egypt,

Jordan, and Syria. In the resulting "pre-emptive" war, Israel more than quadrupled in size and it brought over two million people under new occupation. Yet Israel and its US media allies continue to refer to those events as a "pre-emptive" war or even tell an outright lie by calling it a defensive war. The layman English definition of "pre-emptive" is "to prevent something from happening"; in military terms it means to destroy the ability of the other side to wage war. In 1967, Israel succeeded in obliterating the Arab military forces in the first twenty-four hours of the war. Nonetheless, and for the sake of argument, if we accept at face value the Israeli stance of defining the 1967 war as "pre-emptive", how can Israel reconcile such an assertion with the annexation of occupied East Jerusalem and the Golan Heights from Syria? Acquiring land by force, which was the real intention of the war, is a recipe for more wars, not peace, hence the fallacy of the so called "pre-emptive" war assertion by Israel. The perpetual occupation of land after wiping out the ability of the other side to wage war belied the Israeli contention. Later, American President Bush, and his pro-Israel Neo Cons or Zion Cons, used the same Israeli-invented terminology to justify the ill-conceived war and occupation of Iraq.

The devastation from the air raid on the camp was massive. An unexploded missile I later saw was at least six feet long and about eighteen inches in diameter. The explosions left behind large craters in the field. One opening was about one hundred meters wide and more than ten meters deep. It was deep enough to reach the ground water table. Some of the craters became huge water ponds for many years following the attack.

Whenever my father heard of another Israeli "retaliation", he jokingly stated that Israel always believed in applying the "eye for an eye" principle. It did not, however, matter whose eye they took, they just wanted to get another eye.

Israeli planes and missiles were able to take many "eyes" and, along the way, Israel took part of my childhood memories too, as the green playing field was turned into unsafe craters filled with many unexploded missiles and bombs.

My elder's wisdom has proven correct time and again. Fast forward to May 2006. Palestinian militants attacked an Israeli army post at the border with Gaza and took an Israeli soldier prisoner. Israel "retaliated" to take the other "eye" by destroying Gaza's electrical grid system. As if that was not enough, during a weekend holiday on a Friday in June 2006, parents decided to picnic at the beach with their children to celebrate the kids' good grades at the end of the school year. However, the beach in Gaza, like the playing field in my camp thirty years earlier, wasn't immune from the Israeli revenge attacks. While the families were trying to enjoy their day out, Israeli explosives landed on the beach killing six members of the same family. Since then, more than 1.5 million civilians in Gaza have been under complete blockade – a "near starvation diet" – a policy described by Israeli officials as providing "the minimal requirements for the sustenance of Gaza Strip residents ... without inflicting a humanitarian disaster."

Even when there were no revenge or "retaliation" attacks, there was still the Israeli policy of instilling fear and intimidation by demonstrating its American-made military superiority. I remember many nights when we had to evacuate our neighborhood after Israeli military boats appeared in the deep water alongside the camp's shorelines, or when they sent their military jets to fly low over the camp and break the sound barrier. On one weekend afternoon I was studying for my middle school diploma (another official government exam) on the third floor balcony of the school* when three

---

* Since there was no space to study at home, the school campus was the only quiet place to prepare for the exams during school holidays.

Israeli military jets passed so low above the school that we could see the pilots. The sonorous low-flying jets were a regular occurrence over the camp. I could not imagine any other reason for those jets' loud booms but to frighten the children and to continually remind us that Israel's retributive capability was far-reaching. By the time I was sixteen years old, I had become an expert in recognizing the model of flying Israeli jets and helicopters. But instead of instilling fear in the hearts of the civilians, Israel instilled sufficient resentment for many to be able to justify even the most abhorrent actions against Israel.

I did not realize until I started writing this book that vengeance was deep-rooted in the Zionist psychosomatic philosophy long before the establishment of the state of Israel. In my research, I came across one such indication in a direct quote from the diary of the first Israeli prime minister, Ben-Gurion:

> We need to harm them without mercy, women and children included. Otherwise, this is not an effective reaction. During the operation there is no need to distinguish between guilty and not guilty.[1]

From my own experience, I can attest to Ben Gurion's written words and to the ingrained merciless and malevolent Israeli tactics to "harm ... women and children", a policy that didn't "distinguish between the guilty and not guilty", an Israeli vengeance that didn't even spare animals or plants.

1973 ARAB–ISRAEL WAR

At sixteen years of age, I attended my last school year in the camp, and worked toward graduation from middle school. For this, I had to pass yet another official government exam.

After completing middle school, pupils in the camp had to attend school in Tripoli and merge into the Lebanese schooling system. The school year started in September 1973, and less than a month later, on 6 October 1973, which also fell on the tenth day of the fasting holy month of Ramadan*, the Arab armies of Syria and Egypt launched a coordinated attack against Israel. Several weeks before the war, I had been in Syria with my oldest brother's family when we observed atypical inland heavy traffic of military equipment being hauled from the Syrian seaports of Tartus and Latakia toward Damascus. We, even as non-military neophytes, suspected that Syria must be preparing for war.

In the afternoon of 6 October 1973, around 2 p.m., the BBC Arabic news broadcast announced a coordinated Syrian and Egyptian military attack on the occupied Golan and across the Suez Canal in Sinai. I was at my regular hanging-out place, watching fishermen preparing their boats or fixing fishing nets and listening to the radio. Everyone was elated that finally the two Arab governments had taken the initiative to liberate their occupied land. We speciously assumed the war would also force Israel and the international community to give more attention to the Palestinian refugee problem.

While the camp was not directly attacked by Israel during the war, it witnessed very large Israeli sea assaults against Syrian ports and oil storage facilities across the border. The Syrian seaport of Tartus is located less than eight nautical miles from the camp, on the tip of a large crescent-like bay on the Mediterranean coast. The first week of the war, Israeli warships cast anchor several miles off the camp's coastline and started to pound the Syrian ports and oil storage facilities

---

* Ramadan is the ninth month of the Muslim lunar calendar. During this month, Muslims desist from eating, drinking, and smoking from the early dawn hours to dusk.

in the small town of Banias, near the port of Tartus. We spent many nights on the roof, watching the exchange of fire between Syrian defenses and the attacking Israeli warships. On one afternoon I was at the beach when we saw, in the distance, low-flying Israeli fighter jets coming straight toward the camp. The sight of the fast-approaching shark-like jets with trailing black smoke had us run for cover. Fortunately for the camp this time, the Israeli jets were on their way to attack the Syrian oil refinery on the outskirts of the city of Homs. I am not sure why Israel had to fly its fighter jets off course and precisely over the camp on their way to hit an oil refinery in another country. I suspect they were "killing two birds with one stone", infusing fear and maintaining an unrelenting level of psychological terror against the camp, while on a mission to attack an industrial target some sixty miles away.

Because of America's direct military support for Israel, the Arab gains in the early days of the war were quickly lost. Nevertheless, the war and the level of military assistance needed from the United States proved that Israel was still militarily vulnerable. About twenty days after the start of the war, the Palestinians in the camps were again disappointed with the outcome and with a new peace process that seemed to have totally ignored the refugee's issues. Soon after the ceasefire, I made a political prediction, during a family discussion in our dark and cold living room, that, as in 1967 when Nasser was forced to resign after the Arab defeat, the 1973 war would likely compel Israeli Prime Minister Golda Meir to leave office too. Golda Meir resigned in April 1974, following an Israeli inquiry into the failure in the October 1973 war.

Little did we know at the time that the war had only been intended to "shake the no peace no war" status quo between Egypt and Syria on the one side and Israel on the other. To our chagrin, the war was not designed to shake the foundation of the Israeli occupation of Arab land or to return the refugees to their homes. It was a calculated move by the leaders of Egypt and Syria to simply influence the balance of power in order to improve their negotiating position with Israel. To some extent Sadat was successful, albeit it took a groveling visit to Jerusalem and to have someone like Jimmy Carter in the White House to negotiate a peace settlement between Egypt and Israel.

THE DEFEATED SOLDIER

The war of 1973, which resulted, in my opinion, in another military retreat for the Arab armies, added another dimension to my, by now, more conscious political awareness. While Israel, thanks to US technology, enjoyed overwhelming military superiority, I still wasn't sure how a small country like Israel was able to withstand the advances of the larger Arab armies at a time when Vietnamese peasants were causing havoc for the strongest military power in the world. Some Arab analysts and government apologists blamed the inferior Soviet technology. This was the same "inferior" technology successfully used by rebels in Southeast Asia to rout the American army in the jungles of Vietnam and Cambodia. While technology can play an important role in modern warfare, it cannot be the only determining factor. After all, technology is only an instrument employed by the soldier.

Alas, the Arab soldier was ordained as a tool to protect the ruler, not to defend the nation. The demagoguery of the political tyrants uses all available resources to convince or coerce their subjects into believing that the survival of the regime is the only guarantee of maintaining their national sovereignty. And national setbacks under their leadership, according to them, are only "hiccups" in the long march toward liberation and national freedom. Actually, most of the narcissistic Arab leaders trained and promoted special military forces whose only task was to protect the regime from internal "enemies". This mainly meant to protect the despot from the army that had brought the ruler to power in the first place. Soldiers with great potential or the "cream of the crop" of recruits were lured to special military units whose only task was to protect the one-person system. For instance, the training and arming of the presidential Republican Guards, under Saddam Hussein's regime, was superior to that of the national Iraqi army. The same could be said for almost all other Arab armies where the "national guards" or the rulers' force were typically better trained and financed than the national army. To sum up, the weakness of the nation state perpetuated the degradation of the individual Arab citizen and soldier, leading to ultimate defeat.

For this and various other reasons, the Arab soldier was defeated before the war even started. The Arab soldier, like the Arab citizen, was beaten well before the war by a political structure that denied them a rudimentary role in shaping their system of government. The Arab soldier was, for the most part, a conscript who was forced mostly to serve corrupt and dictatorial political systems. The tyrannical ruling class in the Arab world deprived the individual citizen and soldier of their basic human dignity and hopes in their own country. Loyalty to the despotic regime took precedence over allegiance to serve the country or people. Hence, the humiliation of the Arab citizen and soldier under a foreign occupation was, for the most part, no different from the disgrace imposed by an authoritarian political system. In other words, the Arab soldier did not have much to lose under foreign occupation but to transfer the source of shame from a locally bred tyrannical political system to a demeaning alien occupation.

Furthermore, and subconsciously, the disgrace at the hand of a foreign occupier might be easier for the Arab psyche to bear than the humiliation of a homegrown authoritarian system. In fact, the Arab mind might comprehend, although not accept, the evil imposed by strangers, but find it difficult to rationalize the cruelty of someone with whom they supposedly shared the same cultural identity and values.

For the short term it was more tolerable to be humiliated by an outsider than a local thug. In theory, a foreign occupation brings instinctively a collective resentment toward the outsider, while a local tyrannical political system divides the population between the powerful few and their sycophants on one side, and the suppressed majority on the other. Hence the swift defeat of the Arab soldiers in 1967, and more recently the occupation of Iraq in 2003 at the hand of the Israeli and the American militaries respectively.

The occupation is not, however, the end of the story, as its presence becomes a catalyst for an intuitive united public antipathy against the outsider. Thus, the grassroots revolution and resistance in Palestine and Iraq respectively.

Note

— —

1 Pappé, Ilan, *The Ethnic Cleansing of Palestine* (Oxford: Oneworld Publications), p. 69.

Putting up a tent after a heavy storm, Nahr el Bared, 1951.
(Photograph reproduced courtesy of UNRWA/The Red Cross.)

A childhood photograph showing my brothers and I.
From left to right: me, Majed (standing), Kamel, Ghazi (standing) and Kamal.

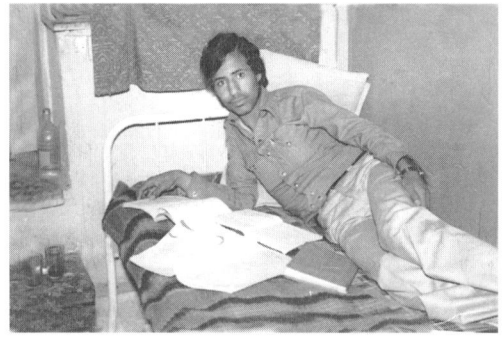

TOP
A family photograph taken in 1965. From left to right: me, my paternal grandmother, Abed el Nasser (on my grandmother's lap), Kamel, Ghazi, Kamal, my father and Majed.

MIDDLE
Studying in my room in Baghdad, 1977.

BOTTOM
Sitting with friends on the shoreline, Nahr el Bared.

Sitting with my family and a neighbor friend. This photo was taken
the night before I left for the United States.

My mother, standing in her kitchen, summer 2002.
(Photograph reproduced courtesy of Doris Bittar.)

Standing with my friend Jim Rauch, in the doorway of my parents' house, summer 2002. (Photograph reproduced courtesy of Doris Bittar.)

A typical classroom in the old UN school, prior to its destruction in 2007. (Photograph reproduced courtesy of A. Waked.)

Celebrating a national day in the main street of the camp, prior to
its destruction in 2007. (Photograph reproduced courtesy of A. Waked.)

Israeli-made ordinance found in the camp
after the fighting in summer 2007.

An aerial photograph of Nahr el Bared taken before and after the 2007 conflict.
Key places mentioned in the book have been labelled.
(Photograph reproduced courtesy of the UNDP.)

Residents evacuate the camp through the south entrance at the start of the 2007 conflict. (Photograph reproduced courtesy of A. Waked.)

The south camp entrance after the 2007 battle.
(Photograph reproduced courtesy of Jamal Krayem Kanj.)

My mother being evacuated by the Red Cross, June 2007.
(Photograph reproduced courtesy of A. Waked.)

The devastated camp, post-conflict in 2007.
(Photograph reproduced courtesy of Jamal Krayem Kanj.)

5

Camp Economy

—-—

The camp's economy had its own cycle, and to a great extent it was independent from Lebanon's economy at large. The camp did not receive any direct or indirect financial assistance or any other services from Lebanon. It was not directly impacted by the level of employment or unemployment in the country. It was an economic island with its own "Gross Camp Product" and to a degree it was not directly influenced by Lebanon's Gross National Product.

In the early years after its establishment, UNRWA was the largest employer and had the greatest impact on the camp's economy. UNRWA employed a large number of white- and blue-collar workers. School teachers were the highest paid staff among UNRWA employees, on average getting paid $200 to $400 monthly. On pay days, the main souk would be bustling with teachers and other UNRWA employees shopping for food and clothing. In later years, a good portion of the camp's income came from the direct remittances of migrant workers to their immediate or extended families.

Legal Palestinian refugees in Lebanon were proscribed from working legally in about seventy occupational jobs. Lebanese labor polices reserved these seventy vocations exclusively for Lebanese nationals or for those with special work permits. These special permits were bestowed mostly on special foreign workers and rarely granted to "permanent" Palestinian resident refugees. In addition, Lebanon, a "confessional democracy" system of government, had idiosyncratic legal statutes intended to maintain a sectarian balance between the seventeen various religious sects. Nevertheless, this policy was not uniformly adhered to when the "Christian-controlled" government in the 1950s and 1960s surreptitiously granted Lebanese citizenship rights to non-Arabic speaking Christian refugees from Armenia. But despite the work restrictions, and to meet the overall demand for certain skilled labor, Palestinian refugees were nevertheless able to work *unlawfully* in many of the banned occupations.

In the 1950s, the camp supplied cheap farm and construction labor to northern Lebanon. In the late 1970s, the camp became a good source of low-priced goods and produce for the neighboring Lebanese community. It later grew to become a competitive regional market for a large number of working-class, middle-class and poor Lebanese and Syrian laborers and nomadic gypsies in the area. The camp enjoyed the presence of indigenous medical clinics, pharmacies, money exchange stores and even communication companies. Gold and jewelry stores successfully competed against the well-established gold souk in the nearby city of Tripoli. With all these economic activities, the community became almost self-sufficient, but was still noticeably impoverished. Despite the economic and financial hardship, it was impossible to find a local street beggar or a homeless person in the camp. The family and social solidarity structure provided a safety net for the needy and the less fortunate. All in all, the camp had the economic balance sheet of a self-sufficient poor country.

Starting in the mid-1970s, the various Palestinian political organizations proffered scholarships for high-school graduates to study in the Soviet Union, Eastern-bloc countries and in Cuba. Most of these scholarships were for engineering and medical schools, hence the relatively large number of medical clinics in the camp. As discussed previously, under the labor policies in Lebanon, Palestinian engineers or medical doctors were not allowed to practice their profession in the country. Still, the Lebanese government turned a blind eye to doctors who practiced medicine within the camp proper or who worked as staff in medical clinics in rural areas. The same went for pharmacists. Palestinians were not allowed to own or operate a pharmacy in Lebanon, but they were able to carry out such prohibited ventures inside the camp. Engineers had less luck, as the demand for this profession within the camp was limited or did not exist. On the outside, it was typical for Lebanese professional institutions (doctors, pharmacists, etc.) to gripe to the government for allowing these professions to operate, but to their chagrin, the Lebanese government refused to enforce its regulations, as long as the services were limited to working inside the camp. Lower overhead costs and profit margins to run pharmacies or medical clinics gave these operations a competitive advantage over the same professional services provided outside. As a result, the vast majority of customers visiting medical doctors or purchasing medicine were from the neighboring communities. This was analogous to US towns bordering Mexico or Canada, where some

Americans crossed the international border seeking less expensive medication outside the United States.

TELECOMMUNICATION REVOLUTION, REFUGEE-CAMP STYLE

In the late 1960s, the Lebanese Ministry of Communication ran underground phone cables through the middle of the camp to serve Lebanese towns and villages in the northern part of the country. Since it did not formally exist on the ministry's maps of areas that required phone services, the camp, even homes or businesses located within less than ten feet of the new lines, were not allowed to benefit from the newly installed phone cables.

While attending college in the United States in the late 1970s, I rarely had an opportunity to talk to my parents over the phone. Occasionally, I called my brother at his office in the city of Tripoli to keep in touch and to schedule a time to talk with my father. For over five years, I did not hear my mom's voice over the phone. The only time I heard her voice or she heard mine was via recorded cassette tapes that I received occasionally with visitors or I sent with someone going to Lebanon.

That changed in the early 1990s as the camp experienced its own communication revolution when ingenuity overtook helplessness. A small entrepreneurial businessman opened a "gray market" telecommunication company. It was even more remarkable that the phone company was established via the island of Cyprus to serve as a communication link between the camp's dwellers and expatriates. Cyprus is approximately 130 nautical miles from Lebanese shores. The small company initially established a landline phone service in Cyprus. It then installed two long relay antennae, one in the camp and another in Cyprus, to manage the incoming and outgoing international phone calls. When this company was first established, expatriates called the phone center to schedule an appointment with their families. The families receiving phone calls were also charged per minute of phone usage. As an example, from the United States the caller would pay the same phone rate as if the call destination was Cyprus, and at the receiving end, the customer would pay another per-minute tariff for phone usage. Basically, the receiving customer paid for the service to deliver the call from Cyprus to Lebanon. Later, with competition from other "copycat" businesses, the competing enterprises started to install direct phone lines to homes. For the new service, subscribers paid a fixed monthly fee for the phone connection and in return they were charged reduced fees for receiving phone calls. Benefiting from the relatively low-cost new service, phone subscribers increased rapidly, which enabled these local companies to provide even more improved benefits, such as building an intra-phone infrastructure network whereby subscribers could reach other subscribers inside the camp at no cost. Several years later, and as the phone services in Lebanon improved, the new telecommunication ventures switched back to a local landline connection from the Lebanese Phone Company. The new business enterprises upgraded their services by acquiring several phone lines from the local phone company to service their main office or the phone hub. From there, an operator would manually connect the calls directly to subscribers' homes. The phone operator was available to transfer calls for about eighteen hours per day. The service was soon programmed, where a recording would ask the caller to enter the subscriber's extension for an automatic transfer. Necessity was the mother of all inventions, and finally, after more than fifty years, this small entrepreneurial ingenuity answered the need and was able to put the camp in touch with the rest of the world twenty-four hours a day.

Other "gray market" ventures included the delivery of satellite and emergency electric power services to residences. Unlike other areas in third world countries where satellite dishes mushroom on roof tops, most homes subscribed to central satellite services at a reduced rate. For the most part, the subscriber's cost covered the cost of the infrastructure wiring system, but not the intellectual property of the service providers. While some of the services may have included special paid satellite programs, most of the TV shows were free-to-air channels.

Emergency power supplemental service was created in response to frequent electric blackouts. Electric service was rationed almost daily in most of Lebanon, and camps usually received the least power, especially during the summer. Lebanon is a tourist-based economy and, as such, the first priority is to provide electricity to tourist destinations, major cities, smaller Lebanese towns, and lastly, Palestinian refugee camps and desolate villages. The frequent power outages in the camp created an opportunity for the small-time entrepreneur to establish small power generation companies to heed the demands for electricity during scheduled and unscheduled blackouts. Power subscribers were provided with a quick connection to switch between the two electricity providers. When the official electric service was out, the local private power generation plant kicked in, and the subscriber received power from the local provider. Overhead phone lines, satellite and power cables navigated the camp alleys between existing power poles like spaghetti noodles, and climbed walls in the small alleys like snakes to reach subscribers.

These were just some of the many examples of the exclusively locally driven initiatives to meet the demand of the local market. These enterprises were initiated and run from within the camp, and were not assisted or directed by outside resources.

NEW OPPORTUNITIES

In the late 1970s and 1980s, money from the Palestinian armed militant organizations became another important source of income for many unemployed young men, and, to a lesser extent, for Palestinian women in the camp. While the new source of income brought short-term relief for several families, it left a long-term negative impact on the overall economic stability of the camp. The political organizations competed among each other by adding youths to their payroll. Youths aged around eighteen were paid monthly stipends for joining one organization or another. The new "welfare-like system" produced a dependent generation that relied on this easy money and lost any incentive to continue schooling or to learn skills at a young age. In the mid-1980s, and as the PLO was forced out of Lebanon, the money started to dry up. Now in their mid-twenties and married, it was too late for these young men to go back to school or to learn new skills. In the short term, the funds from the PLO had played a positive role in keeping the young generation financially afloat, but with its enforced departure from Lebanon, this resulted in a slothful generation that lacked the ambitions or the skills needed for economic survival.

The hopelessness in the mid-1980s brought with it a new wave of migration for the "dependent generation". About the same time, Europe eased its laws for political asylum seekers. A flood of the "dependent generation" departed the camp to seek political asylum in Western European countries. Most of the new migrants went to Germany, Denmark and Sweden, among others. In their new homes, they were provided with financial assistance to start a new life. These new immigrants later became another important source of remittances to help their remaining family members left behind in the camp. Many of my cousins and childhood friends have received political asylum and now live in places like Germany and the Scandinavian countries. This specific new group of emigrants contributed to growth in the building industry at home, as many purchased plots of land to build homes in an adjoining area to the camp. The new neighborhood became known as the new camp. Paradoxically, since these homes were located outside the recognized camp's parameters, the properties had to be deeded by the proper Lebanese government agencies. Furthermore, according to an official Lebanese decree, camp residents were not allowed to own or secure ownership certificates in their names. However, with foreign citizenship, the same Palestinian refugees were able to buy and build new homes outside the camp proper. Expanding outside the original boundary contributed greatly to the overall economy and to the local construction industry in the 1990s.

In the camp, summer was the busy shopping season as many migrants came back from Europe and the Gulf states to visit their families. Like the Christmas shopping season in the West, summer had a similar impact on small shops and businesses. A friend of mine, Mohamed, who had a small money exchange store, told me that his business was usually robust in the summer as the demand on money exchange and check cashing by the visitors became strong. The money flow during the summer did not just come from the visiting migrants, but also from other expatriates who sent money with them to their families back home. Mohamed rented and operated a small space in a pharmacy to reduce his rental outgoings. When our San Diego friend Jim, who happened to be Jewish, his wife Doris and their children visited the camp with us in the summer of 2002, he remarked that the exchange rate at Mohamed's shop was better than what he received in other places in Lebanon. I reckoned the smaller overhead cost and the lean profit margin allowed Mohamed to easily compete with some of the largest established money exchange stores in large cities and towns. The little desk with one chair in the pharmacy was the only available local "bank" to negotiate international notes and a main source for local and foreign currency in the camp.

Mohamed left school before finishing his fourth grade to work as a tailor at the age of ten. He worked in this profession for about fifteen years before changing career to become the main money exchange dealer in the camp. I have sat many hours in his shop, watching him counting and sorting large numbers of bills, adding and subtracting without using a calculator, a daunting task even for a person with a post-graduate degree. More amazing was observing a person with a fourth-grade education closing his accounting books at the end of day with no shortage whatsoever.

By May 2007, the camp was an economic success story among Palestinian camps in Lebanon. Its location on the coastline of the Mediterranean, far from any large Lebanese cities, meant it was not directly impacted by the Lebanese Civil War and gave it a good basis for economic self reliance. Down the years, the camp progressed to become the largest community between the city of Tripoli and the Syrian borders. Its position contributed greatly to making the camp a magnet for wholesale merchants and traders. Although some were involved in illegal trading on behalf of large Lebanese businesses, for the most part the local brokers were hard-working and proved to be competitive against the largest traders in Tripoli. A study conducted by a Lebanese academic found that the camp's industries employed approximately 63 per cent of the local work force. Just before its destruction, the camp was a center of wholesale trading that served most of the areas north of the second-largest city in Lebanon. The camp imported and sold Italian ceramics, cattle from Romania and basic food items. It had at least four regional major tobacco importers. Gold sales and trading thrived, with over thirteen retail and wholesale jewelry merchants. The main road was host to several showrooms of electric and electronic equipment. Along with the commercial enterprises, a derivative service industry developed a new line of employment for skilled trades in electronics, electricity, refrigeration, etc. This was in addition to major medical clinics and about ten elementary and middle schools.

TYPICAL FAMILY STRUGGLE

The economic success did not necessarily benefit all residents. Prosperity benefited mostly the large traders and their Lebanese cohorts on the outside. Besides, not everyone was young enough to be able to learn a skill, or fortunate enough to have a relative living in a foreign place to offer financial support. Men of my father's generation were not apt nor had the basic education to master new skills or the trading market. At that age, men or women were mostly destined for hard labor in construction or farming. I could tell the story of my Uncle Khalid, on my mother's side, who raised eight children working as a daily paid husbandman, or my aunt, my mother's sister, who was killed at an old age by a passing vehicle while crossing the road after a long day of manual farm labor, or my father's lone sibling, Fatima, whose husband raised seven children while working as a daily fruit picker before succumbing to a heart attack. Despite such good examples within my own immediate family, I am instead going to highlight the life of our neighbor Abu Mohammed (AKA Nayef) who made his living as a peddler.

Nayef was about my father's age or a little younger. He owned a mobile shop on a two-wheeled bicycle. The bike was fitted with three small boxes: a box on the rear seat and two boxes hanging on each side of the back wheel. The items and bags for sale dangled from both ends of the bike's front handlebar.

Nayef used to ride his bike several miles a day to craggy remote Lebanese villages and desolate houses around the camp. At times, when the bike was over-laden and difficult to steer, Nayef walked, and pulled it along. His daily travails started before five in the morning or soon after his dawn prayer, and ended around three in the afternoon. He used to target homes that otherwise had no access to close-by stores. People bought from his mobile shop, or if the items they wanted were not available, they specially ordered household items for him to bring back during his next trip. On his day off on Fridays, Nayef carried out his weekly shopping trip to replenish the items sold for that week or to purchase specially ordered items. During the working week, Nayef went to a different area every day; one day he might have covered the area south of the camp, next the area north, and then homes on the east. His entire inventory, including his mobile shop, the bike, was worth less than $150. I am not sure how he made ends meet while raising seven children.

One of his kids was my age; a gaunt, thin boy named Kamel. We gave him the nickname of "the man" after a detective TV show we used to watch with a name translated to Arabic as "The Dangerous Man". As children we used to tease him for being cadaverous because of the lack of nutrition at his home. Kids can be cruel at times. I remember one used to shame Kamel by saying that his mother did not use oil to fry eggs but used water instead. At first, I thought this was made up. But Kamel told us it was true and that eggs can be fried with water and his mother did it because they did not have cooking oil. At home, they raised two chickens and a rooster, which must have been their only source of eggs.

Nayef's dad and his stepmother lived two houses from their home. The older man had at least half a dozen chickens and a couple of roosters. Their yard was fenced with bamboo sticks and rags. The chickens were the only source of income for the elderly couple. I remember numerous times standing outside their yard and hearing Nayef's stepmother talking with or admonishing her chickens for eating too much or for not producing enough eggs, while complimenting other chickens for their good behavior and their plentiful egg production.

Nayef's household was famous for cooking sheep and goat's gut, head and tripe. For some reason, it was not just Nayef who was known for this meal, but almost all the other families that came from the same town in Palestine. The people from the village of A'mka were recognized for having special penchants for this type of dish. Cooking tripe was a sign of thriftiness, but at times it was a delicacy too. Preparing the animal gut was not an easy task. The guts and the tripe were usually delivered fresh from the butcher shop early in the morning. The first task was to empty the digested and undigested food from the animal's internal organs. The tripe was then thrown into boiling water to rid the gut of bacteria and to make it tender. The gut's parts were then divided into separate chunks. The head was toasted and given to the family's patriarch to eat the brain as a delicacy. The tongue was eaten separately, or it could be cut and added to other dishes like stuffed grape leaves or cabbage. The small intestines were usually fried, or if they were large enough, they were stuffed with rice.

When I returned home from Iraq after a nine-month absence, my father bought sheep guts for Mom to cook. As I got up in the morning and saw my poor mother busy cleaning and boiling the guts, I asked her why all the trouble? She said that Dad thought you must be yearning for the tripe after the long absence from home and wanted to celebrate your homecoming. I remember jokingly telling Mom that Dad was using me as an excuse, for he must be the one who was craving the tripe. She agreed. Nayef's wife, Fatima, was a master gut cook. Women in our neighborhood used to defer to her for advice on how best to prepare the tripe.

In later years, and after losing his wife, Nayef became too old and lost much of his strength to propel the bike. I remember telling him years earlier that he must be in good physical condition after riding the bike six days a week. He looked back at me with a diffident smile and did not utter a word. I should have read his eyes though, as they were telling another story about the "exercise" that was taking its toll on his health. I am certain now that he wished he didn't have to have "exercise" on his bike six days a week. After becoming too sick, he converted a small room in his house into a candy and chips store for the little kids in the neighborhood.

Nayef had three daughters and four sons. He never demonstrated a sympathetic attitude toward his daughters. However, when his eldest daughter got married to a person from a remote village in Syria, he could no longer hide his real fatherly caring human side. I understood that his daughter fell in love with a member of one of the militant Palestinian organizations in the camp and ended up marrying this person and moving to his hometown bordering Turkey. Toward the end of his life, Nayef used to visit her about two times a year, even when he was sick. With very limited income, he traveled hundreds of miles to make his eldest daughter feel that she was not forgotten.

In his later days, as his kids were married and had children of their own, they took over the remaining rooms in his house. He started to use his small candy shop as his bedroom at night. Last time I saw Nayef he was very sick with kidney failure and had to undergo weekly kidney dialysis. Since there were no hospitals in the camp, nor could he afford the hospitals in the nearby city of Tripoli, he used to travel two days a week and take two buses and several taxis to the city of Saida in South Lebanon to receive his weekly treatment. The hospital was subsidized by the PLO to offer critical medical services for poor Palestinian refugees. He left the camp on Friday and came back on Sunday or Monday. Nayef used to stay overnight with his relatives who lived in a nearby refugee camp.

Soon thereafter his kidney gave up and Nayef passed away to a more peaceful place, but not before leaving behind the memory of a smile; for he, at all times, even when feeling angry, still managed to wear a genuinely contagious smile on his face.

6

Lebanese Civil War

— —

O n 13 April 1975, the General Union of Palestine Students (GUPS) organized a trip to the cities of Baalbek and Zahle in the Beqaa valley in eastern Lebanon. Baalbek was known as Heliopolis or the city of the sun during the time of the Roman Empire. The city has the remains of one of the oldest Roman temples in the region, built around 15 BC. The imposing marble columns were captivating. We spent the first part of the day touring and taking pictures around the site.

A picnic lunch was planned at a public park on the shore of a well-known river in the city of Zahle, a Christian Lebanese town, often referred to as the capital of the Beqaa valley. This city also has some of the finest and most famous outdoor restaurants in the country. After lunch, the bus passed through the main road in the town and as usual we were chanting

Palestinian patriotic songs. As the bus slowed down for traffic, a person walking down the street was agitated by our chants, made disparaging remarks toward us and started to bang on the door of the bus. We did not think much of it at the time. We always knew, as refugees, that some Lebanese would have liked us to disappear and many on the right-wing of the political spectrum felt threatened by the Palestinians' close relationship with the left and progressive forces in the country. We thus assumed it was just part of the simmering sectarian tension, and also part of the existing tension between the political right and left. The Lebanese National Movement, which was dominated by the left and Islamists, supported the Palestinian struggle, while the predominantly Christian right-wing organizations opposed the presence of the armed Palestinian resistance in Lebanon.

On our way home in the late evening, the bus driver mentioned a news report of a shooting involving a Palestinian bus in Ain Al Rumaneh, a suburb of Beirut. Ain Al Rumaneh was a stronghold of the Phalangist Maronite Christian right-wing party. The targeted bus was carrying Palestinian civilians who were on their way back to Tal el Zaatar Camp.* Half an hour later, the news on the driver's radio indicated that most of the civilians on the bus had been massacred in cold blood. Abruptly the mood in the bus changed from one of cheeriness to gloom, and silence replaced chanting for the remaining hour of the journey. As the bus approached the main road in the camp, we noticed a large number of military personnel walking the streets and traffic was at a minimum. The camp was in complete darkness with a power blackout, which was not unusual. Since we had been scheduled to arrive back late

---

* Tal el Azaatar was razed and many of its inhabitants were massacred at the hands of the right-wing militia during the Lebanese Civil War in 1976.

in the evening, we were surprised at the great number of people awaiting our arrival. My father was there too, and as soon as I jumped off the bus, he gave me a hug and held my hand tight as we walked home. This was odd, for I never expected to be escorted home, nor for dad to wait for the bus, for that matter. I started to worry that something awful may have taken place at home. The mood in the camp was somber. Residents were standing by the alleys, waiting to hear word of the bus's arrival. At home, I walked into a room full of relatives who congratulated my mother and father on my safe return. My aunt kissed me and said how happy she was to see me unharmed. By then, I was dumbfounded; I could not understand what all the fuss was about. It had only been a school outing and a fun day too, until they told me of the rampant rumors in the camp of our bus being the target of the shooting in Ain Al Rumaneh.

13 April 1975 was carved with the souls of the twenty-seven innocent civilians who were murdered that day. The date became the unofficial day of the start of the Lebanese Civil War, which lasted for more than fifteen years.

The Lebanese Civil War brought the country to a standstill, and instituted a formal division between the Muslim and Christian communities. However, the situation was much more complicated than just a sectarian war. Other regional and international factors played a very important role in the internal Lebanese conflict. One, of course, was the participation of the Palestinian forces in the war. The Palestinian involvement was used as an excuse by the right-wing to establish secret relations with Israel, which provided them with training, military and financial aid. Israel used its relationship with the right-wing to redirect the attention of Palestinian fighters from fighting its army in South Lebanon to sinking the PLO deeper and deeper into the long drawn-out quagmire of the civil war. While the Lebanese Civil War had all the signs of a sectarian conflict, it was much more convoluted. Palestinian and progressive Lebanese Christians played a significant leadership role in the Lebanese National Movement and in the fight against the Christian right-wing. This diluted the religious aspect and gave the war a political and ideological dimension.

The war was also described as the 'war of others' in Lebanon. Many believed that Israel was a major benefactor in perpetuating the sectarian divide between Muslims and Christians. Since the early 1950s, Israeli leaders had spoken of the need to establish a Christian entity in Lebanon. Israel believed that a Christian minority state would become a natural ally opposing the perceived Muslim domination in the region. *Diaries*, a book published by the first Israeli foreign minister, Moshe Sharett, revealed that military leader, Moshe Dayan, spoke candidly between 1945 and 1955 of the need to recruit a Maronite figurehead to lead a Christian enclave in Lebanon.[1]

In short, one could justifiably argue that the civil war in Lebanon was down to any and all of the above. There was enough evidence to call the Lebanese Civil War a religious civil war, and sufficient proof to make a case that it was a war between right and left ideologies. Furthermore, there was also sufficient data for it to be classified as a war of others on Lebanese soil.

Some of my friends joined in the fight with fervor to defend the Palestinian revolution. My father used the UN ambulance to evacuate injured fighters and participated in many of the battles in northern Lebanon. Most of the time he was accompanied by his nephew Salah. The nephew seemed to be very much like his uncle, something which my father obviously appreciated. I have vicarious memories of the time during a major battle when many of the injured and dead fighters were brought to hospitals in the city of Tripoli. I went to the emergency room where most of the dead and injured were being brought, hoping not to find my father or my cousin among them. To my sadness, I still saw many young men whom I knew very well, lying in the hospital's makeshift morgue. Some of the young men were college students who had interrupted their studies in foreign countries and decided to come back and join the revolution. A six-foot-tall young man, Mansour, who must have been barely twenty years of age, was lying dead with half of his skull blown away. Others looked more at peace with fatal injures throughout their bodies. In another hospital, in an open yard makeshift morgue, I saw what looked like an inflating corpse of a dead westerner with second-degree burns.

I did not actively participate in the battles, but at times and during calm periods I visited friends at the front. One time, three of us decided to walk to the mountains to visit an active war post, east of Tripoli. Palestinian and Lebanese fighters were entrenched in a missionary school on a hilltop overlooking the village of Zgharta. This post was known as a line of fire or *khat al tamas* between the major sectarian divisions in north Lebanon. We approached the redoubt from the north side and to our surprise we were not stopped by, nor even set eyes upon, any fighters. We walked recklessly toward the main area, exposing ourselves to the snipers from the other side. Then suddenly a fighter appeared from nowhere, screaming and ordering us to crawl on our stomachs. He asked about our identity. We told him that we were looking for friends at the post. After a stern rebuke for walking carelessly in the bulwark's most dangerous area, he told us that our friends were on leave and ordered us to leave the area at once. After realizing what had happened, we were in a hurry to get the hell out of there and went running down the hill toward a safer area.

INHUMANITY

I have plenty of sad memories from the Lebanese Civil War, but there is one specific memory of a childhood friend that has never left me, even after more than thirty years. At a young age I had an orphaned friend named Ahmad Sakina. That was not his formal last name, for Sakina was his mother's first name. Ahmad lost his dad as a child and soon thereafter his mother passed away too. For a short period following his dad's death, he, his older brother and two toddlers were raised by their single mother, Sakina. The four siblings became known as the children of Sakina, hence Ahmad Sakina. Ahmad and I became friends when I was about eight years old. He was a year or two my senior.

Following the demise of their mom, the two young toddlers were placed with relatives in Syria. Ahmed and his older brother were left to care for themselves in one small asbestos-roofed room built for them by UNRWA. Their room consisted of a small closet and two mattresses on the floor. This type of solitary life made Ahmad a tough kid. He relied on his relatives in our neighborhood for food and possibly to wash his clothing. Whenever he visited our home, my mother always exhibited genuine compassion toward him and would always offer him food or drink. He was a very proud kid; he never asked for handouts and would turn down meal invitations. Despite the fact there was no one around to take care of him or his older brother, Ahmad dressed neatly and was always clean, hygienic and immaculate. Whenever we had a fight my mother sided with him, would admonish me and remind me that Ahmad was orphaned and that I must be kind to him.

Like many of the kids in the camp, Ahmad had to leave school at a very young age to support himself financially. Just before the start of the Lebanese Civil War, his older brother emigrated to Germany and Ahmad was left alone in the one-room house. In my early puerile years and as an adolescent teenager, a side of me was envious of that part of Ahmad's life, for he seemed to be free from all parental rules and diktat.

When Ahmed was about fifteen years old, he landed a job as a gas service station attendant in a Christian Lebanese suburb. Ahmad seemed to be very happy in his job. He came to the camp for a visit every other month or so, flaunting his new lifestyle, fashionable clothes and a surplus of cash to spend: he was earning more money than any of us school kids could dream of at that age.

A year later, the civil war erupted in Lebanon and everything changed. Both sides of the conflict committed deplorable and atrocious crimes against people whose only fault was simply being at the wrong place and from the wrong side.

Ahmad was well known as a Muslim of Palestinian lineage in the town. The proud child grew now to become a proud sixteen-year-old young man. According to his co-worker, Ahmad didn't cower when gunmen showed up lurking for him at the service station. He told them, "Yes it is true, I am a Palestinian." He was ordered to accompany them, and when he refused one of the men slapped him in the face. Ahmed, with a strong arm, slapped him back and knocked the armed man to the ground. The gunmen shot him in the leg, subdued and tied his hands behind his back and lashed him to the back of the car. Like a lion in a cage, Ahmad never squealed from his injury nor begged for mercy. He was dragged alive to the middle of town, where he didn't bow his head or even so much as moan before his captors killed him.

HIGH SCHOOL YEARS

For high school education, I attended the same school my oldest brother had graduated from some ten years earlier, an inexpensive local school. The annual cost for the non-profit private school was about $100. UNRWA used to reimburse us for most of the school fees. There were at least three Palestinian educators at this school. These teachers were the most recognized and well reputed in the area. Despite having top-notch teachers, with the start of the civil war, schooling inevitably took a back seat to the flaring conflict. Local schools tried their best to shield students from the effects of war by trying to maintain a regular schooling schedule. Reality, however, frequently intervened.

The students in the school were a mix of Lebanese alongside Palestinian pupils from the two camps in north Lebanon. In English classes, the Palestinians were the majority; nonetheless it was still the first time in my life I had attended a Lebanese school. To save on the cost of transport to and from school, my oldest brother dropped me off on his way to work in the morning, and my father picked me up in the ambulance at home time.

As part of their high school program, Lebanese students had to attend three hours a week of military training. Palestinians were exempted from this requirement. The training was every Monday from 9 to 12 noon with a short lunch break and classes resuming at 12.30 p.m. Since Palestinian students were excused from the training, we had more than three hours to kill every Monday morning. We spent it walking around the streets in Tripoli or going to its small public park. One day we discovered a movie theater with the first show starting at about 10.30 in the morning. The only problem was that the movie theater showed adult movies. Going to the cinema became a Monday ritual for a group of us hot-blooded teenagers. Even some Lebanese students started to skip the military training to come and watch the movies. The show ran till about noon, but sometimes it was longer. At 12.30 we had an Arabic literature class. The teacher was really old, in his late seventies or early eighties. Whenever we got to the class late, the teacher, who knew where we were coming from, would try to embarrass us by asking if the movie had been exciting or particularly hot that morning.

Trying to finish my high-schooling those days was like piloting a plane with no compass, or worse, without knowing the final destination. The official Lebanese government certification system was completely shut down. Students could go to school all they wanted, but there was no official government accreditation to graduate from high school. Even with government accreditation, Palestinian students could not attend Lebanese public universities anyway. The only English-language universities open to Palestinians were two private non-profit colleges, the Arab University and the American University of Beirut. However, studying at the American University was too expensive, and without an official high school diploma, enrolment in either of those two schools was almost impossible anyway. To sum up, to say my schooling during my eleventh and twelfth school years lacked any kind of direction or purpose would be an understatement.

For the twelfth grade I moved to another school, but I still did not receive any real education. It was more like having somewhere to spend the day. One early morning during my twelfth grade, I was showing a 9mm handgun to a school mate when the math teacher happened to walk into the yard. I took the handgun and tried to hide it. The teacher came by and asked to check the gun out. I showed it to him; he inspected it and gave it back to me. I had brought the gun into school partly to show off but also because, subconsciously, I was trying to maintain the city stereotype of the camp's kids being tough. Bringing the handgun was a self-fulfilling prophecy; I was a kid from the camp: a place that purportedly raised hardened individuals. And I had a need to prove that to city boys. Following the encounter, the teacher became very nice to me and I wondered how often he must have thought that I might have a gun on me when he was teaching math. The handgun was my father's, who used to keep it under his pillow. I had taken it without his knowledge and had put it back before he could discover it was missing in the evening. The twelfth grade was the year when I started to seriously contemplate my future, and my way out of the camp.

ISRAELI CLUSTER BOMBS

Before my high-schooling was over, Israeli jets raided the two camps in north Lebanon once again. The other camp, Badawi, was much closer to the city of Tripoli. During the morning school break, in sunny and clear weather, we noticed anti-aircraft bullets exploding behind high-flying jets above the Badawi Camp northeast of Tripoli. The Israeli jetfighters were attempting to raid a well-defended position on one of the hills overlooking the camp. However, with the stubborn anti-aircraft resistance from a three-barrel anti-aircraft gun, the planes were kept at bay and the jets did not dare to come any lower.* We understood that my camp, Nahr el Bared, was also being raided at the same time. We decided to quit school and go home to check on our families and offer our help in

---

* In 1976, Israeli jets did not have the capabilities of firing rockets from afar and had to fly low over the target before dropping their load, especially when the load consisted of short-range cluster bomb rockets.

the aftermath of the raid. Several of us shared a taxi and asked the driver to go straight to the camp.

Upon arrival, I asked the driver to drop me at the bridge, the entrance of the camp and the site of one of the raids. We found out that our camp had not been as lucky as Badawi, as the Israeli planes had been able to hit several targets, including a farmhouse just at the edge of the camp. We arrived at the location soon after the raid and before the arrival of the paramedics. I went directly toward the damaged farmhouse. At the home, kids were crying over the corpse of their father and several people were trying to help. I then ran toward the beach and, as I was running, I passed over a small dead sparrow. I stopped and picked up the dead bird, examined it for a second, and then heard my friend Faraj calling my name for help. I ran as fast as I could to find him standing next to a dead person by the surf. I recognized the dead person lying on the small beach stones as Issa El Eskafi. Issa is the Arabic name for Jesus. El Eskafi was his nickname, which meant 'the shoe repairman' as Issa was the first shoe repairman in the camp. He used to take his morning break every day at around 10 a.m. to walk in the beach area and then duck behind a large pile of stones to relieve himself.* He had laid inert while holding his pants halfway up when he was killed by bomb shrapnel. I picked up his hands and my friend pulled his legs, and we attempted to carry him back to the camp. To our surprise, Issa's body was much heavier than he appeared to be. Later, I learned that dead corpses tend to be much harder to carry than live persons. My friend decided to go and get a stretcher from a

---

* During the early days of the camp, due to the lack of public latrines, camp residents used the coastline as an outhouse or toilets. Issa continued his old habit during weekdays, since the beach was usually deserted.

waiting ambulance. We carried Issa to the ambulance and went back to the bombed field. Several hundred feet from the site where Issa had been killed, I discovered another elderly man lying dead under a thin concrete-covered trench. I recognized this person as one of the elderly men who gathered every afternoon in the same area by the river to reminisce about their past life and memories of Palestine. Among other things, the raid succeeded in ending the daily meetings of these old men.

This time around, Israel had no "retaliation" or revenge to justify the raid on the camp. The air bombardment was not in response to any purported Palestinian attack. Israel introduced us to a new term, for the raid was called this time a "preventative" attack against Palestinian targets in north Lebanon, more than 140 miles from the Israeli borders.

Unlike during previous Israeli air raids, this attack did not leave large craters in the field, nor did it leave behind large missiles equipped with timed delay devices for later activation. The site had instead been seeded with many small bombs. This raid acquainted us with this new weaponry system, called cluster bombs, an anti-personnel system intended to kill and maim as many persons as possible. The bombs were delivered by military jets ejecting large rockets carrying more than 600 baseball-sized bombs in each missile. The rocket acted as a dispenser: it split open into two parts over the intended area before scattering hundreds of the baseball-size bombs over a large zone. Each bomb was fitted with small, twisted wings on the outside making the bomb spin faster while falling over the target. The cluster bomb had four impact-actuated explosive triggers located on four different spots under the thin outer layer. We found several almost-intact half missiles' casings in the raided area. I took an empty half rocket dispenser and kept it in our courtyard as a souvenir for many years.

Another intended and more dangerous by-product of the cluster bomb raid was the presence of a large number of unexploded devices in the field. I didn't realize at the time how dangerous it was to handle unexploded cluster bombs. Along with other kids, I started to hunt for these bombs; I guess we developed an informal program to clear the area of the unexploded gadgets. Children competed against each other to find the largest number of intact devices, so we could blow them up. Since cluster bombs were designed to explode on impact, we would collect the unexploded bombs in a large bag before heading to blow them up on the small rocks by the beach. We took shelter behind a heap of stones after throwing the bombs as far as possible onto the hard pebbles. Most of the bombs used to explode at the first impact. Some, however, did not explode right away and we had to look for them again. It was a nightmare trying to locate the unexploded bombs between the multi-colored and comparable sized rocks. To make sure we didn't lose any bombs that failed to blow up, we had to raise the danger point one notch higher. After throwing the bomb, we would continue to peek from the top of the hiding mound of stones to discern the exact location of the impact, then duck down just a split second before the explosion. Very few of the bombs would malfunction and never explode at all. After several attempts, the cluster bomb got battered enough to split open. At that stage, the explosive sensors located under the outer layer of the bomb would fall out, making the bomb almost harmless. The outer layer was then stripped and the bomb divided into two domes, almost like splitting a baseball into two halves. Each dome was full of what seemed to be solid dry Trinitrotoluene (TNT). Without the explosive triggers, the material was safely removed from each side. After emptying the domes from the explosives, I retained and used them as cigarette ashtrays. They were souvenirs sent exclusively by the Israeli government to our refugee camp. In dissecting the two halves further, we learned more about the killing technology. The internal surface of each dome was carved into small squares. When the cluster bomb exploded, each small carved square became flying shrapnel or bullets to purposely kill and maim as many souls as possible, even a small bird. After learning more about cluster bombs later in life, I just feel fortunate to be still alive to write about one of the most dangerous inhuman anti-personnel weapons ever made, and extensively used by Israel against civilian targets.

THE SUNSET OF MY LIFE IN THE CAMP

Year twelve in school was supposed to culminate with the government's International Baccalaureate One (IB) exam. But since there was no exam at the end of the road because of the war, there wasn't too much studying being undertaken, and the vehicle of my destiny continued to proceed with no end in sight. Meanwhile, the sun started to set on my life in the camp as the school year was coming to a close. Before my eventual departure, I had to deal with four important episodes that marked my last full year in Lebanon.

In the summer of 1976, facing the Syrian military pressure against the camp and the ongoing Lebanese Civil War, the PLO decided to institute draft military service for young Palestinians. Earlier in the year, the Syrian government had sided militarily with the right-wing in fighting against the Lebanese National Movement and their Palestinian allies. The Syrian army, supported by Arab governments and with implicit approval from Israel and the US administration, had entered into Lebanon to save the right-wing coalition from certain defeat and to halt a victory by the Lebanese National

Movement. In response to the new threat, the PLO ordered the recruitment of all young men who had completed their high school education. The first enlistees were picked by a lottery, and the names were announced on loudspeakers throughout the camp. As luck would have it, my name was called in the first pick. We were instructed to report to duty by next morning. I got up early in the morning and bade farewell to my mother and went for the waiting bus. The response to the call was very good, with at least 60 per cent answering the call for duty. The bus was full of seventeen- and eighteen-year-old young men, with people standing on the side of the road to bid us goodbye. The bus took us to a military training center in an olive grove next to the Badawi camp. The base was prepared to welcome the new recruits with a set of tents and beddings. To our disenchantment though, other than the tents and sleeping quarters, there was no real military training program. The first day after our arrival, we were given instructions on how to clean and take the AK-47 apart, which we already knew. The program on the following day included physical exercise with a long jog around the military base.

By the third day we realized that there was no program and the whole draft was a joke. Many of the guys decided to abscond from the base or simply walk out. My oldest brother, who had not wanted me to go in the first place, drove with a rebel captain from Fatah by the base and asked me to jump into their car. To their disappointment, I refused to go and decided to stay at the base. By the end of the week, the base had only four remaining recruits out of more than forty who had answered the first round call. At that point we were released by the base leader and sent home. Having received almost no military training, the whole episode felt more like my first camping experience in an olive grove than an induction into a military career.

AIRPLANE HIJACKER

During my junior high school year, 1974–75, I got to know a very quiet student with the last name of Mi'ari from the Badawi camp. Mi'ari's physical features seemed to be more western than typically Arab. He was blond with blue eyes. I did not know at the time that he had any political affiliation, other than being a sympathizer with the Popular Front for the Liberation of Palestine (PFLP). All Palestinian students tended to support one political organization or another. We used to find out about every one's partisanship during the annual election for the General Union of Palestine Students.

Following Arafat's famous speech at the UN General Assembly in New York, Mi'ari noticed the picture of Yasser Arafat and Fidel Castro on the cover of my chemistry book. He made disparaging remarks about Arafat being a sellout for going to the UN. The picture of Arafat and Castro had been taken during his visit to Cuba after the United Nations speech in 1974. While most Palestinians supported Arafat's UN visit and the speech, some in the radical left rejected the visit as a futile effort in the face of Israeli intransigence and its continued refusal to recognize the plight of Palestinian refugees. I got into a little disagreement with Mi'ari over the UN initiative. He said that while he agreed with the gist of Arafat's speech, he thought "it was pointless as long as Israel, cosseted by the US government, continued to reject the recognition of the Palestine Liberation Organization as the sole representative for the Palestinians and to deny our rights as a people for self determination." He went on to say that "it was despicable for someone who was oppressed in Europe to justify taking my home in Palestine and to make me a homeless refugee." Israel, he said, "will only return what is rightly ours when it becomes too dangerous for the Israelis to remain in our homes, not by a speech at the doors of the UN."

About two years later, Mi'ari transformed his genuine frustration into action. In 1976, he took part in a plane hijacking carried out jointly with a pro-Palestinian German group. Mi'ari, along with the Germans, boarded an Air France flight en route from Tel Aviv to France with a stopover in Athens, and diverted the plane to Entebbe, Uganda. Several days later, he and the German hijackers were killed in a famous Israeli commando raid at the airport. Since the hijacking had been sponsored by a small underground PFLP splinter group (Wadi Hadad), there was no official announcement in the camp about his involvement in the hijacking. His family did not even hold a mock funeral. This was typical for loved ones who died fighting the Israelis when their bodies were not repatriated to their families. Actually, every one, including his family, found out about his involvement in the Entebbe hijacking almost a month later, when posters with his picture on were secretly distributed at night in the camp by the underground splinter group. Mi'ari was killed at the age of nineteen, the age when normal kids usually start college!

SUICIDE ATTEMPT

At that age, I was one of a very close group of six or seven friends. The Lebanese Civil War was heating up and life's prospects did not seem too promising to any of us in the camp. One of my friends, Hasan, was from the neighboring Badawi camp, stationed in Nahr el Bared as a fighter with one of the local paramilitary groups. This organization was sponsored and was closely associated with the Iraqi regime and therefore was reviled by the Syrian government. Out of the overall group of friends, three of us were particularly close, the core of the group. There was basically nothing to do but find ways to kill time. After my special early morning snorkeling in the sea, the group used to get together mid-morning to spend a couple of hours walking around the camp, drinking tea or coffee. Then we met again in the afternoon, went to the beach or played cards. Hasan got into a disagreement with members of the core group and as a result he was boycotted by everyone. In the meantime, Hasan and I continued to maintain at least a superficial relationship. Like with almost all my friends, I was the youngest of the group. They all were at least a year older, and Hasan was about three years older. Hasan was at the stage in his life where, like us, he did not see much of a prospect in the future, but possibly much more so for him since he was the oldest. He was very depressed, not that I knew what depression was at that age. He was having a difficult time at home, with his unit and now with his friends. One morning we were hanging around the UN ration center, which had been rebuilt after its previous destruction by the Israelis, watching the old people receive their rations. Hasan, in his regular green fatigue and holding an AK-47 on his shoulder, came by and asked me if I wanted to go for a walk. Even though he seemed pretty tense, I did not suspect anything unusual and neither did any of my friends. We walked for about 300 yards, I still have no recollection of what we might have discussed at the time but I felt he just needed someone to talk to about our problems. Then he stopped and with a smile he opened my right hand and gave me a piece of paper. I tried to glance at the written note, but before I could open my hand, he held onto my fingers to keep my palm closed. At that point, I became suspicious that something bizarre was going on, especially as I noticed him turning his gun toward the right side of his stomach and smiling as though it was his last grin. I then attempted to open my hand again, but it was too late. He pulled the gun's trigger, resulting in a loud gunshot, and then fell to the ground. Everyone around the public place heard the bang and came running. I asked him why? He continued to smile but said nothing. I carried him with a friend who arrived in no time to a nearby clinic, about 700 yards away. He was given emergency first aid and was driven in an ambulance to a hospital in Tripoli. We stayed at the hospital until after his operation and after he had been placed under observation. Hasan was in a critical condition during the first night. Fortunately for him and for me, he survived the incident. We were all lucky that there had been a clinic close by; otherwise he would have certainly died from internal bleeding.

Even though Hasan had only completed elementary schooling, his suicide note was more than telling. In the short terse note, he lamented about life as he quoted a line from a famous poem by a renowned eleventh-century Arab poet, Abu al-'Ala' al-Ma'arri. The line states: "My life is a peccadillo I inherited from my father, and life I intend not to pass to new progeny."* The note went on to say that he had had enough of life in the camp, "For I want to belong and in this life I do not belong." He asked for forgiveness from everyone and said he looked forward to seeing us in a "place where we all belong".

---

* Al-Ma'arri was born in Al Ma'arra near Aleppo, Syria. He lost his sight at the age of five due to smallpox. He was a foremost free thinker, never married, known for his intellect and his cynicism of life. Abu al-'Ala' articulated his thinking about religion in a poem:

They all err – Moslems, Christians, Jews, and Magians
Two make Humanity's universal sect
One man intelligent without religion
And one religious without intellect

After I left the camp, I lost contact with most of my friends (but for those who stayed in the camp) until Hasan phoned my home in San Diego in 1999 from Denmark. I found out that he had spent several years in a Syrian jail for his membership of the Palestinian organization. After his release he traveled illegally to Europe, applied for and was granted political asylum in Denmark.

THE LAST SWIM

In September 1976, the Mediterranean was at its finest. The weather was still warm and the sea was at its calmest period of the year. I started to borrow a spear gun from my best friend Imad (he was killed in 1983), got my snorkel, an inflated inner tube and went fishing every morning. The snorkeling was just off the neighborhood in a rocky area about 500 yards from the coastline. There were very few fish at the time. The area had been rich with cod, rock bass and eel before the destructive dynamite fishing was introduced. During that period, I used to run into a fish or two and some eels. It must have been seasonal, for immediately following the hot summer months, there seemed to be more eels and octopuses than during any other period. Eels were unpredictable creatures that did not fear humans like fish did. For that reason, eels were easier to shoot with the spear, as one could place the gun close enough to the eel before releasing the lance.

Another interesting encounter was with an octopus during a time when I went dynamite fishing on the rock area outside the camp. This type of fishing was carried out by free snorkeling, without a boat or an inner tube. A stick of dynamite and box of matches were held by raising the left hand above the water while the snorkel was submerged almost all the time underwater. I had to swim by paddling with one hand and both legs. Swimming with one hand while raising the other above water was exhausting and, for that reason, I swam close to an atoll of small rocks to stay close to a dry area if I needed to rest. While snorkeling, I felt something touching the edge of my bare heel. I took a look backward with my head still submerged in water, to see a good-size octopus with its legs spread and approaching my foot with the suction cups wide open. I was terrified as I swam fast with both my arms and legs and made a dash for the island. After climbing to safety, I looked down and there it was sitting on the rock's reef. I stared down at it, and the octopus gazed back up at me. The dynamite stick and box of matches were wet and useless. I stood like that for a long time before I dared to jump into the water from the opposite side of the rock to swim back to safety. I am not sure how much harm an octopus could have done, but those days we believed in fictional tales about a large octopus's super ability to hold swimmers under water with its suction cups while gluing its other legs to the sea bottom, thus drowning the swimmer.

On an early October day in 1976 after my morning dive, I went home to find out that the sun had finally set on my life in the camp. There was a ship leaving Tripoli seaport that afternoon, and I was to be smuggled to Baghdad via Cyprus that same evening.

Note

1   Edward W. Said, *The Politics of Dispossession*, p. 45.

7

Journey into a New Life

— —

The Mediterranean Sea served as both a renewable reserve of food and income to many in the camp, and an indirect source of inspiration for my future outlook. I remember far back when, following heavy sea storms, we roamed the shorelines scavenging for the bountiful troves washed up by the waves. Just as the early bird gets the worm, so, soon after a major storm, people would line the beach trying to recover items of interest: young men would collect washed wooden boxes and children would seek out plastic toys. The beached plastic toys would come from a washed-out landfill in the city of Tripoli some ten miles south of the camp. Heavy sea storms would flood the landfill, pulling the garbage into the water and in the process cleaning the toys, among other things, before depositing them in our area. At the time, I naively speculated that the toys had been thrown into the water or been accidentally dropped by rich kids on cruise ships docked at the nearby refinery. Our area was familiar with the sight of large oil tankers berthed at the refinery south of the camp. At that age I couldn't distinguish between a cruise ship and an oil tanker!

The sight of large ships arriving at and leaving the refinery left a lasting subliminal impression on my future outlook toward migration. Almost daily, I was attracted toward the sound of the oil tankers' loud toot announcing their departure. Whenever the blaring horns were sounded, I looked toward the ships and wondered if and when I would one day ride a big boat and disappear beyond the horizon.

The day when I would get that chance finally arrived in October 1976. A month earlier, my oldest brother Ghazi, without either my knowledge or my acquiescence, had submitted my last school year's grades to a local official from the Iraqi branch of the Ba'ath Party.* This was as a means of applying for me to matriculate at a Baghdad high school. Because of the continuing civil war in Lebanon, the governmental educational system had been shut down. I thus had a choice between going to Baghdad to finish high school or staying and lingering around the camp. Upon learning of the submitted paper work, I did not give it much attention at the time, for I was aware that a group of students from the camp had already left for Baghdad in early September and I assumed it was already too late in the school year to enroll and travel to Iraq. In the second week of October 1976, my brother indicated that my school documents had been accepted by the Ministry of Education and I should start getting ready to travel. His local contact advised him that

---

* Iraq was governed by the Ba'ath Party. Ba'ath, or 'Renaissance' in English, was a pan-Arab nationalist party founded by Michael Aflaq, a Christian Arab, in the 1930s.

once in Baghdad, I should check in with a special governmental office that handled school matriculation for incoming Arab students. I was told that the office would help with the school and possibly with accommodation. Since the school had already been in session for over a month, I was advised to leave for Baghdad as soon as possible in order to be able to catch up.

In 1976, Lebanon's civil war was reaching its climax, the only airport in the country was closed, and with Syria siding with the Lebanese right-wing militia, travel for Palestinians via Syria was severely restricted. To complicate things further, Syria was ruled by a splinter Ba'athist faction which was at odds with the Iraqi party branch. The two "presumably Arab" countries were political adversaries. Hence, land travel from Syria to Iraq was not possible. The only other available option to reach Baghdad was to travel by sea and then fly to Iraq via a third country. At the time, the harbor at the city of Tripoli was a very busy port for sea trade between Lebanon and the city of Limassol in Cyprus. However, sea traffic was limited for the most part to cargo shipping between the two ports, mostly importing contraband goods into Lebanon.

I had just returned from an early morning fishing and snorkeling escapade when I was informed of a cargo ship scheduled to depart Tripoli's harbor later that afternoon, for which I needed to get ready to leave within an hour. My mother had already started to fill a suitcase with all of my belongings. I was told to meet my oldest brother, Ghazi, in Tripoli, where he was making the arrangements to smuggle me out of the seaport. Since it happened so fast, I did not get the chance to say goodbye to any of my friends, relatives, or even to some of my own brothers. I kissed my mother's hand, asked for her forgiveness, and to be less conspicuous, I took my last ride in the UNRWA ambulance to Tripoli.

Security restrictions at the harbor precluded male youths, especially Palestinians, from traveling through the seaport. As the civil war was at its pinnacle, and as Syrian army pressure against the camps was worsening, military groups had issued a travel moratorium on all young Palestinian men of military draft age. On the departure day, Ghazi secured a special pass from the head of security in north Lebanon. The local security personnel also provided contact information for help while in Cyprus.

At the seaport, we discovered the departing ship was still emptying its cargo and would not leave until late in the afternoon. We had plenty of time before boarding and my dad decided to go back to downtown Tripoli. It was the first and last time I got to spend quality one-on-one time with my father. He invited me to a sweet shop and ordered a cake called *kenafah*. *Kenafah* was made of cheese or rich cream soaked with homemade rosewater syrup. I didn't like the *kenafah* much and I had rarely eaten it before; however, on this special occasion I made an exception and ate nearly all of it. After the sweet shop, Dad took me to a watch store and bought my first expensive wristwatch, a Seiko. It was priced a little over $50, a very large sum for my dad's salary. The watch was the only thing bought in preparation for the trip and I kept it for more than fifteen years. My dad didn't say much that day. While he appeared a little tense and worried, he seemed to be pleased that I was leaving to finish school, evading the civil war and possible military service. I understood later that he was very apprehensive about the trip and wondered if I was ready to leave the nest. He confided in me many years later, "It was like pulling a tooth [without anesthetic], while very painful instantaneously, it healed with time."

I had no contact information in Iraq, not even an address for the incoming students' office. I knew only of the group of about four older students who had left for Iraq several weeks earlier, but did not have the means to contact them once in Baghdad.

When the time came, I kissed my brother and kissed my dad's hand and jumped into a small dinghy waiting to take me to the cargo ship in the middle of the harbor. I presented the special security pass and was waived in without questioning. I handed my suitcase to the crew and climbed the rope ladder onto the ship. On the deck, I glanced back into the boat below and felt as if I was leaving my soul behind; at the same time, however, I felt my spirits soar at the thought of the adventures that lay before me.

Aboard there was a small crew and very few passengers, including one young woman. On the lower level, I noticed a semi-raised tent covering the open hatch of the empty cargo area. It was almost the end of day and the sun was setting behind the water. From afar, I saw my dad and brother waiting on the dock for the ship to sail. The ship engine ran for about an hour before receiving clearance to depart from the port authority. By that time, it was getting dark and I could not see my dad or brother any more, but I was confident they were still anxiously standing at the waterfront. When the ship started to move, I stood on the side deck to wave goodbye to the dark shorelines, and I was certain that someone was waving back.

I am not quite sure how I felt at that very moment, but without a doubt I was confounded. I had realized long ago, as a Palestinian refugee growing up with five other boys and one girl, that I was being groomed to be the first child in the family to leave the dead-end life in the camp. It hadn't been that long ago when I had stood on the beach and turned toward the tooting oil tankers leaving the refinery south of the camp and wondered, if and when, I too might get to travel on one of those ships disappearing into the mysterious horizon. The day had finally come, but instead of an oil tanker, it was a cargo ship. I shed no tears bidding farewell to loved ones, but my eyes, like the moon's reflection on the surface of the Mediterranean water, were sparkling pale as the ship started to sail. Sitting with the few passengers outside the engine room at the rear of the ship, I took one last glimpse at the camp about ten seafaring miles to the north. It was a small patchy spot of diminutive lights. I thought of my mother, my father and siblings and wondered how my mother was doing, seeing my dad coming home without her son.

The sea voyage between the cities of Tripoli and Limassol in Cyprus took about ten hours. Three hours into the trip, the shoreline lights started to fade away. I had finally arrived at the "mysterious horizon"; it was an eerie feeling. There was gloomy water and dark skies everywhere, but for the company of the moon and the stars. Like a fledgling bird, I understood at that very moment the need to learn how to fly solo or else be doomed to fall flat on my face. Taking the first jump was not easy. Sailing into the unknown darkness was frightening. I started to close one dark past chapter of my life as the ship steered into yet deeper darkness. I hoped to start opening a new chapter, a new life and future for myself and for those whom I left behind in the camp.

By midnight, I was getting tired and went looking for a place to sleep for the night. There were no sleeping quarters for travelers, barely enough bedding for the crew. I carried my sole piece of luggage and descended to the covered area at the lower level. I pulled the side of the tent's tarpaulin and pushed my suitcase inside. The only woman passenger on the ship had already taken cover under the tent, and she was shaken observing me crawling down. I tried to assure her by pushing my suitcase to the other side of the tent. Exhausted after a long day, taking the cold wooden floor as a mattress and my suitcase for a pillow, I closed my eyes and tried to snooze for the remaining nighttime hours.

About four in the morning, the ship suddenly came to a standstill and an intense light shone inside the tent. I went outside to take a look and saw a number of large military vessels in the vicinity, but no sight of land. I asked a crew member about the military ships. He indicated they were US craft patrolling the Mediterranean and were inquiring about the ship's cargo. He requested that I remain on the lower deck as the American vessels had not been made aware of civilian passengers on board. Moments later, the ship received the green light to proceed toward Limassol. I couldn't go back to sleep and decided to stay up on the top deck.

As the daybreak drew nigh, the sun started to rise from behind the sea: a complete reversal of my habitual daily sunrise ritual where the sun rose from behind the mountains, and at dusk disappeared into the sea. With the sunrise shining from the rear of the ship, the city of Limassol started to appear far in the distance.

Approaching the port of Limassol, the ship waited its turn for permission to enter the harbor. Several hours later, Cypriot immigration officers boarded the ship to inspect the passengers' identities and to issue entry visas to Cyprus. When my turn came, I was questioned about the purpose of the visit. I requested a transit visa for my planned onward travel to Baghdad. They asked for proof I had money to cover my stay and the cost of travel to Iraq. I had about $500, enough for a one-week visa stay in Cyprus and for the airline ticket.

Outside the harbor, I had no idea where to go. I shared a taxi with some passengers and together we went to the same hotel. Upon arriving, I noticed that the hotel had been either a school or a small apartment building before being converted to an inn. I shared a large room with three other travelers. I spoke very little English at the time, but the local manager of the hotel spoke good Arabic with an Egyptian dialect. Next day, I needed to find my contact in Cyprus to help with the travel plans to Baghdad. I asked the hotel's manager how best to reach him. The manager called the person, who gave me directions to his office. It transpired that this person worked in a travel agency where a ticket was booked for me on the Royal Jordanian airline (Alia) flight departing Larnaka Airport in three days time. The small Larnaka Airport was a replacement for the main Nicosia Airport that had been shut down following the Cypriot–Turkish War two years earlier.

I spent the next three days eating one meal late in the day, surviving on bread for breakfast and lunch. On the second evening, I discovered an inexpensive eatery that barbequed meat skewers on the sidewalk. The third day, I told the men with whom I shared my room about the inexpensive restaurant and asked them if they wanted to go for tasty barbequed meat. The price was interesting and they decided to join me at the eatery. Just by looking at the meat, my room-mates suspected it was pork and not lamb as I had professed earlier. The restaurant owner confirmed my room-mates' suspicion. I was embarrassed; needless to say that night I didn't have any food. I must admit, the meat tasted no worse than lamb, but when I discovered it was pork, like the others, it was a turn-off. I joined the young men for a walk in the town. The guys were about ten years my senior and were very familiar with the city streets. They knew the location of all the nightclubs, bars and even the brothels. We arrived back at the hotel room before midnight so I could pack my suitcase in preparation for the next day's flight to Baghdad. My companions were returning to Lebanon on a cargo ship the next morning. I asked if they would deliver a letter to my parents, and they agreed. I spent about an hour writing the letter, describing my trip and the planned flight to Iraq the next day. In the morning, I gave them the letter with a phone number to contact my brother's office in Tripoli. Months later I found out that the letter was never delivered and my parents were not aware of my whereabouts for several months. I will come to that later in this chapter.

BAGHDAD

In the late afternoon of the next day, I checked in for the Royal Jordanian flight to Baghdad with a stopover in Amman, Jordan. In those days, and possibly still today, the Royal Jordanian airline was known to have security personnel on board the plane. In Amman, some passengers disembarked and new ones came on board. A young man in his early twenties took the center seat next to me. I introduced myself and found out he was from the occupied West Bank, on his way back to university in Baghdad. This was the first encounter I had ever had with a fellow Palestinian from inside of Palestine. When the plane started to take off, in an expression of hostility toward the Jordanian monarchy, I made a remark to the extent that I was happy the plane was finally leaving the polluted place. I was still incensed with the Jordanian government for the events of September 1970, when Palestinian fighters had been forced out of Jordan after a long, bloody war. The person sitting next to me did not utter a word. He may have suspected I was a potential mole for security trying to fish out unfriendly passengers. Actually, he didn't even talk much until the plane started to descend into Baghdad's airport. He asked about my destination in Iraq. I explained to him that I too was a Palestinian from Lebanon and planned to attend high school. He asked if anyone was picking me up upon arrival. I told him that I knew a group of students from the camp but had no idea how to reach them. Feeling sorry for me, he indicated that he lived in a one-room apartment and I was welcome to stay at his place for the night. He offered to take me to the Palestinian student union the next day to try to connect with the other students from the camp. This person was a godsend, for I hadn't been sure *what* to do, having arrived in Baghdad late at night. After picking up our luggage and clearing customs and immigration, we took a taxi to his place. He sat in the front and I took the back seat. On the way to his flat, I listened to him talking with the Iraqi driver in the local accent, which at the time I did not comprehend well. It was totally Greek to me.

His place was literally one room with a small balcony and not even a kitchen area. He had one small bed. He offered his bed and took the chair to sleep for the night. I must have been either too tired to resist or just simply selfish, as I accepted his invitation, jumped on the bed and slept like a baby. I don't think he slept much on the chair that night, as he was up really early in the morning making tea and emptying his suitcase. We drank tea before taking public transportation to the neighborhood of Al Waizariah in Baghdad. Al Waizariah was a middle-class neighborhood known for the large number of student union offices. We walked into a large open yard in a house-like building. It was the General Union of Palestine Students, Baghdad branch. I was happy to walk into a place and see a number of Palestinian students, mostly college-bound. Inside, I asked if anyone knew of Palestinian students from Nahr el Bared Camp. I was told that someone from the camp was staying at Algiers (Al Jazza'er) Hotel on Al Rasheed Street. We took my suitcase onto another bus, and off we went to Algiers Hotel. The hotel's front desk directed us to the room for people from the camp. The god-sent individual felt I was now in good hands, shook my hand and bade me goodbye.

He was yet another human being I had run into by chance and never got the chance to thank properly for his help. Worse still, I don't even remember his name. Several months later, I saw him walking affectionately with an Iraqi girl. He looked toward me but ignored my presence as he was probably embarrassed. I looked back and in deference to his feelings I did the same. In our culture, it can be awkward for an unmarried man and woman to walk amorously in front of a person they know.

The Algiers Hotel was at best a rundown one-star or not-even-rated hostel. The rooms were small, about eight feet by ten with three single beds: one bed at each of the three sides and a sink on the fourth wall next to the door, with no closets. The floor's common bathroom and showers were located at the end of the hallway. I shared the room with two guys from the camp who were seeking work in Iraq. One person had finished his accounting diploma and the other had completed his teaching credentials at an UNRWA institution in Lebanon. They were very kind and treated me like a little brother. The other kids from the camp were staying with their older brothers who were already going to university in Baghdad. The hotel was very inexpensive, less than half an Iraqi dinar per night. An Iraqi dinar was about $3 at the official bank rate, but much less on the black market. One of my new room-mates landed an accounting job for about thirty-five dinars a month. The other room-mate was doing odd jobs while still looking for a permanent teaching position. After several days, another group of students from the camp arrived and were able find a room in the same hotel. School was already in session and we needed to go through the office of incoming Arab students to be assigned to a school campus. The office was much politicized. Students with good party connections (i.e., with the governing Ba'ath Party) had the best chance of getting into a good school and receiving special assistance.

I was a year or two younger than all but one of the other students from the camp. The older students had finished their thirteenth grade in Lebanon, and were hoping to start at the university level. The two of us younger students had completed only twelfth grade and were hoping to get into the last year of high school. As we waited to hear from the office, the older students were informed that since they had not received an official Baccalaureate diploma (IB) from Lebanon, they could not be admitted to university. They needed to finish high school in Iraq before matriculation at university. This was bad news for all of us, for we were also afraid that we, the younger students, might not be allowed to attend the last year of high school. Days later, we were given the good news of being assigned to the graduating class and were advised of the school to attend. The best news, however, came when the incoming Arab students' office announced that we had also been granted a place in a school dormitory in the Al Adamiyah district. All in all, it was a big relief.

I was still at the hotel when a university student from the camp came to visit with urgent news. He had received a letter from the camp asking about me, as my parents had indicated that I had left for Baghdad over three months earlier but lost all contact with the family. I found out then that my parents had never received the letter sent from Cyprus and did not know if I had ever made it to Iraq. I was distraught with the news, as for all this period, I had assumed that my parents had received my letter, and would have known of my travels to Baghdad. The news could not come at a worse time. Because of the ongoing Lebanese Civil War, there were no direct communication lines, no phones and no telegrams between Iraq and Lebanon. My only option was to write a letter back via a third country, which usually took several weeks to arrive. The letter had to be sent via a PO Box in Tartus, a coastal city in Syria near the northern Lebanese border. From there, the mail was picked up by someone from the camp, who in turn delivered each letter to its intended recipient for a small fee.

The mail business was one of the first gray entrepreneurial businesses in the camp. With the start of the civil war, an industrial businessman rented a PO Box in Tartus to enable people in the camp to correspond with their loved ones outside Lebanon. A working line of communication with the outside world was very critical for many of the camp's residents. To some people, especially the elderly, financial remittances from loved ones overseas was the only source of income for their survival. However, sending a letter via Syria from Iraq could have personal political repercussions. Mail between Iraq and Syria was closely scrutinized by the security services in each respective country. Even worse, any individual sending and receiving mail was placed on a special suspected list by each of the security services. And, since letters between the two countries required "special handling" by the security services in each country, it resulted in a serious delay to an already inefficient mail delivery system. Nevertheless, the comfort a letter might bring to my parents was more important to me than any political consequence; hence I immediately wrote a letter and sent it via the Syrian PO Box. Several months later, I received back a hand-carried letter brought by someone from the camp, in which my dad described his relief upon receiving my first mailing. In his reply, my father stated that the postman had come running with a big smile on his face to tell him of the "letter from your son in Iraq". Since my dad couldn't read, he ran to my oldest brother to get him to read it for him. The letter from my parents cheered me up no end and made up for the worrying of the previous months.

I did not send or receive another letter via Syria again. During the school year, I might have received three letters and maybe sent about the same number back again. The letters were mostly hand delivered by someone traveling to Baghdad or by another who was going back to the camp. This was the case when I sent my second letter in January 1977 with the ex-room-mate from the hotel. The person with the teaching credentials gave up trying to find a job in Iraq and decided to go back home. That letter also brought joy to my parents for another good reason. It was typical of people from the camp to visit with their compatriots before going back and to ask if anyone wanted to send letters or money (in the case of working individuals) to their families. My old room-mate came to visit us at the dormitory while I was studying outside in the yard. I wrote my letter in a hurry and gave it to him while he waited. As soon as my former room-mate arrived back at the camp, my dad went straight to visit him, inquiring about me and asking if I had sent any mail. After receiving the letter, my dad could not help but ask about school. My ex hotel room-mate explained that when he had visited the dormitory on Friday, a school holiday, he had found me studying hard outside my room. He complimented my father on my behavior and told him how he should be proud of his son. My father could not have received any better news, for I usually was the kind of student who always needed a little prod to study, especially at weekends.

The students' dormitory was a large three-story building. It housed mostly Arabs, north and sub-Saharan African students. My floor consisted of two large halls. Each hall housed about twenty students, and had twenty dividers with a walkway in the center. Each division included a bed, a two-door metal cabinet and a small standing area with a sheet-covered door for privacy. The closet was enough for my small set of clothing, books and non-perishable food items I kept in my room. The two large halls connected with a lobby area, leading to the shared bathrooms and sinks. The building did not have any showers. The lights in the sleeping quarters were turned off by 10 p.m. Since I did not have or could not afford a personal lamp in my area, whenever I needed to study past 10 p.m., I would have to go downstairs to a study area located on the ground floor.

I was assigned to a school in the neighboring Al Kadmiyah district across from the Tigris River. Every morning we had to walk about a mile to reach the main road to take public transport to school, and walk a similar distance from the bus stop to the school. At the school, I was treated kindly by teachers and students alike. I was not made to feel a stranger and everyone in the school was willing to help. The Iraqis were one of the most proud and considerate people I have ever met. As a sign of special treatment and for the first time in my life, I was seated in the second row in the classroom. I had to adjust to learning math, physics and chemistry in new Arabic terminologies, as I had initially learned all those terms in English while schooled in Lebanon.

Around December 1976, we were informed that because of the continuing hardship, all students from Lebanon were to receive a monthly government-issued stipend of eighteen Iraqi dinars. It couldn't have come at a better time, because by December, I was running out of cash. I had no bank account, and the official mail from Lebanon was so unpredictable it would have been difficult if not impossible for my parents to send money. Considering that we had free housing and free schooling, the eighteen dinars was a generous sum to cover the cost of food and transportation. The monthly allowance insured that I could survive without money from home for the duration of the school year. Up until then, I had been able to survive by being a little frugal. I didn't leave the dormitory at weekends. During school days, a low-cost falafel sandwich was enough to fill me up for the whole day. On Tuesdays after school, I would run to the grocery store in our neighborhood hoping to buy eggs and plain yogurt, if available. Tuesday was the day when subsidized eggs and yogurt were distributed in very limited portions to the store in our neighborhood. If lucky, I would find a couple of eggs and one small yogurt container, enough to feed me for two or three days. If not, I bought canned sardines. I would eat half of the can with lots of subsidized cheap bread at lunch and eat the other half at dinner. After receiving the allowance, life and food improved. I started to eat out more often, mostly at hole-in-the-wall type eateries, and was able to go to the theater to watch a movie every once in a while.

I was very skinny at the time, but even so I lost a lot of weight and became gaunter. Part of it was being homesick. Apart from when I had run away six or seven years earlier to join the revolution, I had never been away from our house. At home, I was excessively picky when it came to food. I must have driven my mother up the wall complaining incessantly about food. I would not eat food if it was oily, I would complain about food if it was too salty or not salty enough … The very food I complained about at home, I missed dearly in Baghdad. Once in Iraq, I experienced a complete turnaround by eating all kinds of food. If I was invited over for a meal, which I would have turned down even when I was hungry in the camp, now I gladly accepted the invitation, even if I was full. Being away from home was also a turning point in my appreciation for a home-cooked meal and for food in general.

While I got over the cooking part by eating all kinds of dishes, I did not get over my homesickness. I was so desperate that I conspired against myself in the hope to have the Iraqi government deport me from the country. I made blatant and disparaging remarks about the Iraqi president Hassan Al Baker and his then vice president Saddam Hussein, thinking that if the Iraqi government heard about this, they would kick me out of Iraq. I guess the walls did not, after all, have government ears, as we had previously been led to believe. Time did not necessarily make it any easier. The hardest part about being away was the lack of direct contact with the family in the camp. I had no access to phone calls or regular mail.

In about January 1977, during a lull in the Lebanese Civil War and when the postal system in Lebanon was working, I received a telegram from my parents after a car bomb exploded in a crowded civilian area in the city. Baghdad was a large city, and I am not sure what the odds were of being hurt by a car bomb in such a large place; however, that was typical of my father. He was a worrier and it was his way of saying, "We love you and are thinking of you." I don't recall sending a response, but I must have communicated back one way or another.

When I arrived in Baghdad, the weather was very pleasant and I didn't know what to expect of the summer. I was taken aback by how cold it got in December and January. The sleeping hall had no heating system, thus making the nights freezing cold. Each room or divider was assigned two light blankets. One blanket was placed on the top of the mattress as a sheet cover and the other was for cover when sleeping. During the two cold months, I used both blankets to cover my whole body, including my head. As far as I remember, it was the only winter ever when I did this. Nahr el Bared Camp was much colder than Baghdad, but even there I had never needed to cover my head to maintain a warm body. Ironically, sharing a bedroom with seven siblings brought some warmth in the camp, but this didn't happen in a large open hall in Baghdad. Early in the morning, I would see shivering birds outside the window warming up in the corner of the building. Walking to the bus was taxing. I had one heavy sweater and a hat to cover my cold ears on the way to the bus stop. The classrooms did not have heaters either. However, the weather was more bearable during the day and with as many as forty students in the class, the room warmed up fast.

There was no hot water at the dormitory building. The water was too cold even to wash one's face. The only hot water was in a public shower located next to the main building and available one day in the middle of the week when the water was heated for a couple of hours. The shower room was large, steamy and crowded with young students taking the weekly shower and washing their garments. Again, even in the camp with the lack of water and heating, I had much better hygiene than I did during the months of December and January in Baghdad. In the warmer months, we were able to clean and wash our clothes in the bathroom sink at the dormitory.

About February 1977, several of us from the camp formed a theatrical group. I have no recollection of how it came about, but an Iraqi Palestinian who had acting experience and theater education started to work with us to direct a short play and also to practice on a musical piece. For the political play about the life of Palestinian prisoners in Israeli jails, and I did not know why, the director picked me to play the role of an Israeli prison guard. We rehearsed three times a week after school on an open-air podium near the dormitory. In March and during national and pan-Arab festivities in Iraq, we were invited by local schools to present our play.

We were also practicing at the same time on a musical presentation for a song by the famous Lebanese singer Fairouz, titled *Longing for Jerusalem*. Staged after the Israeli occupation of Jerusalem in 1967, this song became one of Fairouz's signature pieces. The song's music and the poetry were very powerful. Whenever I hear that song, even now, I still remember the day when, more than three decades ago, we stood on the stage marching and pounding our feet on the theater's floor to the sound of the music and lyrics. We put on such a good performance that the group was asked to present the musical on the stage at the University of Al Mustanseriah, the second largest university in Baghdad. With a large mural of the Dome of the Rock at the center stage and to the sound of music and Fairouz's chants, a group of Palestinian students from a refugee camp in Lebanon moved the audience to a standing ovation.

The short play and the musical were my only extra-curricular activities while in Baghdad. It kept us busy for about two months and brought the new friends from the camp closer together. Soon after these activities, we didn't have much extra time on our hands as we started to prepare for the national high school exam.

One cannot live in Baghdad and not acquire fond memories of the place. After all, Iraq was a cradle of human civilization. I think it was in Baghdad where I developed a lifelong special appreciation for old buildings and old neighborhoods. And Iraq had it all.

At the time, the Iraqi government was also looking toward the future, as they zealously promoted education, self-reliance, industrialization and manufacturing. Learning was becoming an important pillar in Iraqi society. Another program, although less successful, was the government's push to improve productivity and services. Motivational slogans were displayed at public offices, promoting hard work and calling for better customer service. I doubt the government achieved much success in the latter two areas.

I would have loved to spend time visiting different places in Iraq, but due to my limited financial resources, my life centered on the immediate neighborhood. Nevertheless, I got the chance one night to wander around outside Baghdad. A relatively well-to-do Iraqi student mate, with access to his family car, a Volvo station wagon, invited a friend from the dormitory for a trip to two well-known national historical and religious sites. I was invited to go along. It was the beginning of summer and we were done with the school finals. We left in the afternoon and visited the city of Samarra, where we climbed the famous spiral tower and visited Shia and Sunni holy mosques in the city. Our mate was a member of the Shia sect of Islam. From Samarra we drove south to the holy city of Karbala, where we visited some of the holiest places for Shia Muslims. The dazzling night lights and colors around the holy shrines were stunningly bright and beautiful. The place was crowded with pilgrims from all over Iraq and the world. As we drove back to Baghdad after midnight, we had time to discuss the differences between Shia and Sunni Muslims. This trip was my only venture outside Baghdad and I cherish all the memories, especially as we watch the current sectarian strife perpetuated and stirred by the ill-fated invasion of Iraq.

After completing the IB exams, I couldn't wait to go home. The airport in Lebanon was open during another lull in the civil war. I had saved enough money from my monthly stipend for a one-way air ticket to Beirut. Since it was difficult to contact my parents to let them know of my trip, I decided on a surprise visit. After arriving at Lebanon's airport, I shared a taxi to the city of Tripoli and another to the camp. I still remember reaching home, carrying my suitcase, pushing the outside door with my foot to surprise my mother who was sitting inside and looking toward the door as someone was barging in without knocking. Her beautiful smile is forever imprinted on my memory as she saw me walking in. I was the first son who had lived away from home for that long. Her fledgling bird had just flown back to the tree.

Three weeks later, I found out that I had to go back to Baghdad to retake an exam for one unit. I went back and spent most of the summer of 1977 in the city. I was tested in late July or early August, but had to stay until the official results were announced to pick up my official IB diploma, which meant lots of free time. In 1977, the fasting month of Ramadan fell during August. The students in the dormitory stayed up all night and slept during the day. It was my first Ramadan away from home. Ramadan is a special month for the family as my poor mother spends most of her day cooking several kinds of dishes, lots of greens, salad, soup and desserts. My fast-breaking in Baghdad was limited to one type of food, usually the dish of the day at the small "hole in-the-wall" restaurant I visited every evening. However, since we slept most of the daylight hours, the fasting part was effortless. As for Ramadan sweets, it was made up by eating lots of sweet unripe dates. Unripe dates are picked from the tree when they are still yellow and before they turn dark. I prized eating the unripe dates during that Ramadan, and Iraq then produced among the best dates in the world.

I enjoyed the relatively cool summer nights in Baghdad. As time allowed, I would go in the evenings to Al Adamiyah's small public park by the Tigris River. People would walk by, or sit on public benches to eat seeds, have a soft drink and listen to Arabic music on loudspeakers. For me it was time to reflect on my life, miss home and listen to emotive songs by Abdul Halim Hafez, a renowned Egyptian singer, on the kiosk's speakers.

Iraq has polarized weather. As cold as it got during December and January, it was the other extreme starting May and June. To cool down the dormitory hall, an archaic air-conditioning system was placed at the entrance door to blow air. Essentially, it was a fan drawing air through wet straw. A water hose was connected to the air conditioner to keep the straw wet. When the straw was wet, the air conditioner or the "evaporative cooler" blew cool air into the room; but the minute the water hose was disconnected, it became hot recycled air.

Toward the end of August, the IB results were announced and I started to get ready to go back home. Still though, and to collect the official certified IB diploma, I had to call on multiple locations for the Ministry of Education and then to other government offices for official certifications. The weather was extremely hot, and having to dare, along with thousands of other Iraqi students, to get the bureaucratic stamps and certifications made it that much more difficult. By the end of each day, I had to take multiple buses back, without air conditioning, and get ready for the next day. During the day, the only functioning cooling system was to perspire profusely to regulate the body's internal temperature with the outside heating system. After several days, I succeeded in picking up a complete certified diploma and was on my way back to the dormitory. During the ride I started to contemplate life in general and Iraq in particular. I considered whether I would be coming back to finish college in Iraq. I reflected on the extreme weather and pondered about the first people who had inhibited that land. How were they able to endure such climatic extremes?

Then, thinking as a Palestinian, I wondered if the ruthless climate was what had actually compelled Abraham, the progenitor of the three monotheistic religions (Judaism, Christianity and Islam), to leave the realm of Mesopotamia (Iraq) for the land of Canaan (Palestine) around 2000 BC.

Approximately 4,000 years later, in August of 1977, I too left Baghdad, and my journey to America started to take shape as the bus approached the dormitory for the last time.

8

A New American Home
and the Return to Palestine

--

The journey to my new American home started with an awkward introduction to the unique American holiday of Thanksgiving. On the fourth Thursday of November 1977, my oldest brother Ghazi came looking for me at the beach to tell me to get ready: we had to leave for Beirut right at that instant. When I asked why I was told: "We have received your college acceptance from a school in Texas, and we need to go to the American embassy to apply for a student visa." Just like prior to the boat trip to Iraq the year before, I jumped into the car and off we sped to the Lebanese capital. The diplomatic mission was located on a beautiful waterfront property* in Ras Beirut. When we arrived it was completely deserted but for the security personnel, who advised us that the mission was closed for two days in observance of the Thanksgiving holiday.

The following Monday and before daybreak, my father and I were in the queue waiting for the embassy to open its doors. After a brief physical security check at the hands of US marines, we entered the waiting room at the counselor section. About an hour later I was called to the interview window where I presented my I-20, college acceptance, financial affidavit and my high school diploma to the counselor. The embassy official asked me several questions, but seemed to be most interested in finding out why I had been in Iraq and what I had done there. "To finish my high-schooling due to the civil war in Lebanon," I told her. She kept my travel document‡ and the other supporting affidavits and directed me to come back in the afternoon. I was informed by others in the waiting room that this meant she was inclined to approve the travel visa, for otherwise she would have rejected the application on the spot.

My father was very anxious as we walked back and forth along the beautiful promenade by the beach. At the designated time, embassy staff called my name and handed me the travel document with a student visa to the United States. On the way back, my father kept emphasizing to me the importance that I work hard: this would be my only opportunity to leave a life of catastrophe. If need be, my parents would take food out of their mouths to help me succeed in my new life.

I left the camp for my new home on 1 December 1977. Life in the States was rewarding for me and eventually for the

---

* This embassy building was destroyed in the spring of 1983 by a truck driven by an apparent suicide bomber.
‡ Palestinians living or born in Lebanon were issued special Palestinian refugee travel documents.

people I left behind. I supported myself in part by working at various fast food establishments and at gas stations – in one of which, incidentally, I was held up at gun point one early Saturday morning. My siblings and parents joined together to help with the cost of school tuition and when I was between jobs. Notwithstanding all the above, in addition to the FBI and other local enforcement agencies' displeasure at my political activism (it was at college in the States where I was introduced to political activism and student organizing), I graduated as a civil engineer in 1983, became a California-registered Professional Engineer years later, before going back to night school to complete an MBA in Global Management in 2001.

The story of my life in America, the challenges, successes and setbacks at both personal and professional levels deserves much more than a chapter in this book. For this reason and to avoid a long excursion into another worthwhile topic, I have elected to keep the focus of this book on life in the camp and on the journey that led me to the United States. While my life in America was a story of immigration by choice, the lives of those in the camp were stories of forced dispossession and long lives of catastrophe which affected more than five million human beings.

After nineteen years in my new home, my wife and I decided to take our two boys (as they were then) to look for our buried roots in a place we had never visited nor would ever have been able to visit before we became US citizens: Palestine.

TEL AVIV AIRPORT

In November 1996, I was invited by a UN agency for a job interview in the Gaza Strip. The job was to manage

European-funded projects for a new water and sewerage system for the refugee camps in Gaza. This area had recently been returned to the Palestinian Authority as part of the Oslo-negotiated peace agreement between Israel and the PLO. Justifiably, I was excited at the opportunity to "return" and help the fledgling new nation, especially as it would involve improving living conditions in refugee camps similar to the one in which I grew up.

The UN civil service system has several classes of fixed term or temporary employees, each with a different local or international category. The recruitment was for international staffing, which meant a salary package at least five to ten times the level of compensation granted to equally qualified local recruits. The UN arranged for my flight from San Diego to Tel Aviv and for local transportation from the airport to Gaza. After a flight of more than five hours from San Diego to New York, I traveled on the now defunct TWA Airlines on a non-stop flight from New York to Tel Aviv. I was very apprehensive about this voyage, and the more than twelve-hour flight across the Atlantic did not make it any easier. For the first time, Hebrew was the predominantly spoken language in my surroundings and in the cockpit. Even though I had lived in an area less than 150 miles from the border, this was my first ever trip to that part of historical Palestine. Since I was not able to fly into the Palestinian-administrated area, the plane had to land in Tel Aviv and I was not happy about having to submit to an Israeli authority in order to visit Gaza. Other Palestinian Americans had already cautioned me about the "special treatment" Arab-sounding names received upon arrival at Tel Aviv Airport.

The TWA flight touched down early in the afternoon of a nice sunny November day. The plane landed far from the airport terminal, which meant we had to be transported by bus to the main building. Travelers were for the most part excited at arriving at their final destination. I, on the other hand, was getting more and more tense, knowing that this was just a mandatory intermediate stop on my way to Gaza. Passengers soon lined up to exit the plane and descend the flight steps. Waiting in the queue by the exit door, I noticed two plain-clothed Israeli security personnel at each end of the stairs' landing. The security personnel with dark sunglasses were scanning passengers as they disembarked. I was half-expecting, as I had also been forewarned, to be pulled to one side for questioning before being allowed onto the bus. I ignored their presence completely, however, and confidently continued to walk down the steps and onto the bus. I had passed my first test either by acting insouciant, or perhaps I may just have looked to them like the many arriving Israelis and/or Jewish passengers. I knew, however, that things would not be so easy once inside the terminal, as my name and place of birth would be revealed as soon as anyone examined my passport. During the bus ride, I braced myself for customs before taking my place in the queue for foreigners waiting for their turn at the immigration counter. As I handed over my passport for inspection and an entry stamp, I asked the officer not to stamp my passport, since I would need a "clean" passport for travel privileges into Lebanon; anyone with a stamped entry into Israel was barred from traveling to Beirut. The officer, who seemed familiar with such requests, agreed to stamp the Israeli visa on a separate piece of paper. After my passport had been electronically checked, I was issued a different color pass along with an entry visa. Next to the customs booth, another officer was in charge of inspecting visas and collecting the separate passes. The color of the pass determined whether or not further scrutiny would be needed before the passenger was allowed to leave the airport building. I turned in my pass and again tried the same act of walking past the guard. It did not work this time, unfortunately, and the security man asked me to step to the side. He radioed other security personnel for the "special" handling. The security officer took me to the luggage carousel to identify my baggage. He handed me a cart and asked me to bring my bags to a corner office. On arrival, he put on disposable plastic gloves and started to feel the bags from the outside. I didn't understand what was being done at the time. However, later, through my trips into and out of Gaza, I came to learn that they rubbed their gloves against the suitcases to pick up possible bomb residue. They then ran the gloves through a special machine that senses even the minutest level of bomb powder or other remnants (e.g. flower pollen) that might be confused with bomb powder. To the side, I noticed a person who looked like a Palestinian sitting on a bench. While awaiting the glove test results, I asked him to tell me about his situation. He explained that he was from the West Bank and was coming home for a visit: he had to go through this "meaningless" interrogation before he would be allowed to continue his trip home. He expressed his yearning for the day when he would be able to bypass this "annual ritual of humiliation" just for the privilege of being able to visit his own home. I asked him how long the procedure usually took. He responded, "Not to worry about me, I may sleep here tonight!"

I guess I was surprised when the officer came back, handed me my passport and asked me to take my luggage and leave. I was already incensed by the "special treatment" and asked the officer, "What about this guy, when is he leaving?" He responded sarcastically: "Is he traveling with you too?" "No, but I would be interested in finding out as I may be able to give him a ride," I responded. By then the officer had started to get agitated and he snapped, "If it was not for the American passport, I would have been more than happy to keep you in the company of this 'creature'." I was livid by then and would not have cared even if I had been sent back. Without thinking, I moved my right hand from the cart and instinctively gave him the finger. His face changed color like a distressed octopus; catching a grin from my fellow 'creature', I dashed with my cart to get out of his face as quickly as possible. I left the other powerless Palestinian on the bench waiting for an Israeli officer, quite possibly foreign-born, to grant the "native" Palestinian permission to go to his own home.

Inside the arrival hall, I saw a lady carrying a sign with my last name. She was an international UN driver who, unlike local Palestinian drivers, was able to travel in and out of Gaza and the West Bank. International drivers were also paid substantially more than the equally qualified local Palestinians.

On the drive from Tel Aviv to Gaza, just before sundown and sitting in the back of the minibus, I began to enjoy the scenery of the land outside. I barely talked to the driver or the other traveler who had been picked up from an earlier flight. I had grown up visualizing Palestine's landscape and its beauty. I had been raised believing that this land had been stolen from my parents and all the people in the camp. I caught glimpses of sparse older fruit trees, the likely remnants of what were once established farms, the topography and the land contours with cactus plants denoting the vestiges and natural boundaries of old villages. For a moment, my memory took me back to the circle of old men sitting by the river in the camp reminiscing about their life in this land. Meanwhile, and as the sun started to disappear beyond the horizon, the car continued to drive along the Mediterranean coastline which I had dearly missed for nineteen years.

Soon there was a rude awakening as we arrived at the Israeli Ertz checkpoint on the border with Gaza. The driver asked us to disembark from the car for the Israelis to check our passports and visas before we crossed the heavily militarized checkpoint. It was getting dark as we drove into Gaza. My immediate impression of the place was that it was like a large refugee camp in Lebanon, but with accessible roads instead of alleys. There were few if any functioning street lights, roads were haphazardly built, and it just did not have the feel of a city. I arrived at a newly built hotel on the beach. I checked into my room and was ready to sleep after the long flight and terrible jetlag.

Early next morning, a local driver came by to pick me up for the scheduled interview at the UN building. I walked into a room with a panel of two men (one American, the other English) and a woman (European, possibly Austrian), but with no local representation on the interview board. Following the interview, they asked their local Palestinian driver to give me a sightseeing tour of the Al Shati refugee camp. This area was one of the several refugee locations that needed new water and sewerage systems. I immediately felt at home in Al Shati Camp: it reminded me very much of my camp, back in Lebanon. Both were located right by the Mediterranean Sea. Like in my camp, I saw firsthand the dire need for a working water distribution and sewerage collection system. I knew I wanted the job the minute I realized how much I could contribute to improving the life of residents in the camp. The road along the shoreline brought a fresh breeze mixed with the stench of untreated sewage discharging into the open sea. The sound of the gently breaking waves brought back strong memories of the beach where I had dug sand and collected animal bones to supplement my allowance as a child. I saw the spirit of that young boy in the souls of the children hopping over running sewage in the alleys of Al Shati. Similar to the name bestowed on my camp, Nahr el Bared, after the cold river, Al Shati means "beach" in Arabic.

Following the tour, I was driven back to the office and then to the hotel in preparation for the late evening trip back to San Diego. Around dusk, the international driver arrived for the two-hour drive back to Tel Aviv Airport. Meanwhile, I had different plans in mind. I decided to visit the West Bank and the holy places in Jerusalem and Beit Laham (Bethlehem) before departing for California. In the hour or so I had after my interview, I enquired privately with the local UN travel coordinator about a good Palestinian hotel in East Jerusalem where I might stay for couple of days. I called the airline and postponed my travel accordingly.

Unfortunately, because of the shortage of time and my lack of familiarity with local transport, I decided not to go into the Galilee area to look for my father's cousins. I did not have an address or a phone number and was not sure how big the town was, or how hard it would be to locate their homes. Besides, I had never met them before and felt it would be a bit odd to just go there and introduce myself as the son of a cousin they had not seen or talked to for the last forty-nine years. However, and as discussed later in this chapter, destiny had other plans.

JERUSALEM

Vehicular transportation in and out of Gaza was limited to UN cars, international UN employees and some VIP personnel from the newly established Palestinian Authority. I kept my plans secret from the UN agency and the driver who was to drop me at Tel Aviv Airport later that night. The local Palestinian transport coordinator advised me to take a minivan (*sheroot*) from Tel Aviv Airport to Jerusalem. As we left, the international driver seemed keen to find out if I understood any Hebrew. I suspected she was a dual Israeli and British citizen. It would not be a far-fetched conjecture to assume that she could have worked also as an informer for the Israeli government. On the way to the airport, and after she was assured that I spoke no Hebrew, she made several phone calls where she conversed only in Hebrew. We bid each other goodbye at the departure lounge, but instead of going to the airline ticket counter, I went to the arrivals exit, looking for the minibus or "*sheroot*" parking. The waiting *sheroot* for Jerusalem was half full. I had just turned in my suitcase and taken my seat when the driver enquired about my destination in Jerusalem. I gave him the name of the inn, the Holy Land East Hotel. After hearing the hotel's name, he got a little sulky and I did not understand his problem. After all, I was a paying passenger and he was certainly content with that part at least. When the *sheroot* was full, the driver collected all the fares and off to Jerusalem he drove. It was late evening and the road to the holy city was dark with very few bright street lights, so I was unable to see much of the landscape. Approaching the city, we passed by a very well-lit area of what seemed to be old historic military vehicles in a park-like setting on the median strip and on the right side of the highway.

I came to understand later that this monument was down the hill from the site of one of the massacres committed by Jewish terrorists against peaceful Palestinian villages. While the Palestinian community ostensibly enjoyed the protection of the British mandate power, Zionist armed terrorists launched an attack in the early morning hours of 9 April 1948 on the village of Deir Yassin: according to UN investigation reports the Jewish Irgun organization, under direct orders from Menachem Begin, slaughtered a large number of the Palestinian civilians in the village.

To justify murdering women and children, Begin explained that "The massacre was not only justified, but there would not have been a state of Israel without the victory at Deir Yassin."[1] Ironically, Begin, who once headed the British authorities' "most wanted" terrorist list, later became Israeli Prime Minister and was awarded the Nobel Peace Prize. The staging point for the launch of the massacre was later turned into a national Israeli commemoration park to celebrate one of the Zionists' most triumphant campaigns to depopulate Palestinian villages.

Once in Jerusalem, the driver dropped the other passengers first in what looked like Jewish neighborhoods in the city. This was manifested by affluent housing and a meticulous infrastructure support system with five-stars hotels on hilltops, sidewalks, street lighting, roads, etc. I knew I was on the Palestinian side when all that disappeared. I was the last to be dropped off as the driver did not seem to be familiar with the address of the hotel. He made several calls to the front desk for directions. I recalled at that point the driver's apprehension when I told him about my destination while at Tel Aviv Airport. He must not have been comfortable going to East Jerusalem, the Arab section of the city, and it was very obvious that the driver was not familiar with the Palestinian area. Taxi drivers are universally recognized to be the human equivalent to GPS satnav when on the road in their own cities. Like the Israelis, I am certain many white South African drivers would have been equally challenged driving into black neighborhoods in Johannesburg during the apartheid era.

At the hotel, I checked into my room on the second floor. After throwing my hand luggage onto the bed, I immediately went to open the curtain to check out the outside view, if any. When I opened the blinds, I caught the most magnificent view possible from a hotel room. In the midst of the darkness, directly ahead, was the shining golden Dome of the Rock and the Al Aqsa Mosque on the one side, and the brilliantly-lit Church of the Holy Sepulcher on the other. I have seen pictures of the same view countless times on posters or the TV, but it was real this time, and just across the street from my hotel room. I stared long and hard at the old city wall and back to the golden dome, at the mosque, and then back to the church.

I was getting hungry, having arrived just past midnight. I asked the hotel attendant if there was anywhere in the neighborhood I could get some food. He sent me to the empty main street next to the old wall, where I found a *shawarma* sandwich shop. I bought two chicken *shawarma* sandwiches and a soft drink, and went back to my room. With the nicest view, I sat down and finished my dinner while admiring the glory of the old city. I attempted to get some sleep before embarking on my exploration of the city the next morning. However, I felt like a little child who couldn't sleep thinking about the morning Eid or Christmas gifts. I woke up really early and ventured outside the hotel. The streets were empty. I crossed the main road and stood by the usually bustling but now deserted gate of the old city. It was too early in the morning and the only sellers out there were the newspaper vendors. I bought a newspaper and went back to my room. As soon as I had finished reading the paper, I went down to the main hotel lobby for a cup of coffee before a second attempt to visit the old city. By now, the morning sun was shining and vendors had started to bring their goods to sell to tourists.

Finally entering through the gate of the old city, I was emotionally overwhelmed as I walked on the old stones and along the ancient standing walls. I was actually walking in the very neighborhood where Christians believed Jesus was crucified, on the same stones the Muslim Arab leader Omar Ibn Al Khatab had walked upon, and along the same walls the Muslim warrior Saladin had liberated from European crusaders. At that moment I understood what it meant to be part of an old history, an old culture, and a rich civilization. I finally discovered the depth of my own roots buried deep in the ground of the old city. I wanted to hug the ground and kiss the walls, if only I could. I sauntered without any clear direction. I knew I would eventually run into a holy place, but I was still enthralled just at being there. I was mesmerized by the several thousands of years of abrasion and marks left upon the stones by pilgrims, warriors and tourists. I, too, wanted to leave my mark, as I rubbed my feet hard along the stones.

My fascination with the history of the place was short-lived as I soon found myself facing an Israeli military checkpoint in the middle of an old neighborhood. After they examined my passport, I was allowed to continue walking into a large open area. On the left side, I saw the Al Aqsa Mosque or Haram Al Sharif. On the lower area, Jews were praying at an ancient wall face. The wall is revered by both Muslims and Jews. In Judaism, it is believed that the wall is a remnant of Solomon's temple, and is referred to as the Wailing Wall. Muslims, on the other hand, call it the Al Buraq Wall, the site where Prophet Mohamed ascended to heaven. I walked to Haram Al Sharif from the gate designated for tourist visitors, otherwise known as Bab Al Magharibah. The Haram has a large, beautiful courtyard with an old wall enclosure of the mosque and the Dome of the Rock. I noticed a sun dial clock on the top of a small, arched wall up the stairs that divided the Dome courtyard from the main lower level Mosque area. I took several photos of the wall and the clock. While standing by the wall taking a picture of the Dome, I observed a small group of tourists with an Israeli tour guide. I could not help hearing the tour guide's political proselytism and his demeaning remarks about Palestinians. I confronted the tour guide and admonished him for his misrepresentation and asked him to stick to his job as a tour guide on the third holiest Muslim site. He ignored my remarks and just asked the tourists to follow him and moved away from where I stood. When I complained to one of the unarmed Muslim guards at the site, I was informed that Israeli government regulations did not allow Palestinians to work as official tour guides, not even at Muslim or Christian sites, and these jobs were reserved only for Israeli Jews.

From what I had previously seen in photographs, I had high expectations of the place's grand design. From the outside, the Dome looked stunning and seemed like an architectural masterpiece. Still, that was nothing compared to the majestic magnificence of the view inside. Oh! What a rapt structure! It reminded me of my first visit to the Grand Canyon: while I had seen photos of the site before, the awe of looking down the Canyon's chasm was beyond description. I had a similar experience looking up the underside of the Dome and at the mosaic on the walls. I was spellbound by the artwork and entranced by the resplendent craftmanship. To think, unlike the Grand Canyon, this place had actually been built by human beings! I took plenty of pictures, even in areas where photography was not allowed.

I left the Dome and went to the Al Aqsa Mosque in the lower courtyard of Haram Al Sharif. I took off my shoes, as I had at the Dome earlier, and walked inside the third holiest site in Islam. Muslims believe that Al Aqsa Mosque was originally built during Prophet Mohamed's era. The name "Al Aqsa" came from the Prophet's description of a mosque that was built in a very far off place. In Arabic, the name "Al Aqsa" means "the furthermost point". My fondness for old structures was obvious as I sat on the carpet admiring the roof and enjoying the mosque's interior design. I was moved and inspired to be in the place where Muslims believe Prophet Mohamed rose to heaven after leading a group prayer of all God's messengers. And for the first time in many years, I decided to pray for having the opportunity to visit Palestine, my native soil. My prayer was not one of the five mandated daily rites for Muslims. It was a thank you prayer. For that I did not follow the same obligatory ablution required when standing before God for regular prayers; it was the thought that counted.

Muslim authorities administering the site banned picture taking after a Jewish terrorist attempted to burn down the mosque in 1969. The attack resulted in substantial damage to what was known as Saladin Altar. Like all Jewish terrorist attacks against Palestinians, Israel dismissed the attacker as a "deranged individual", a legal code label to evade accountability and set the stage for the eventual pardon or the early release of the Jewish terrorist.

Unlike inside the Dome of the Rock, however, the mosque was not very crowded and taking pictures would have been easily noticeable. I had two cameras on me, one with black and white and the other with color film. While sitting on the carpet, I took several photos of the inside without looking through the lens, hoping that some of the pictures would be worth keeping. Alas, I never found out. The cameras were lost or destroyed a day later.

At the end of the day, I went to a nearby post office to mail a postcard of Jerusalem back to my office in San Diego. Having been highly impressed by the engineering feats of the old city, I wrote on the card that "After seeing old Jerusalem, I realized that we engineers were new kids on the block."

Old Jerusalem left me with a new appreciation of the engineering profession. Civil engineers typically concern themselves with how functional and cost-effective their work is, while architectural engineers are creative dreamers to a certain extent. As a result, there is always an underlining professional tension in the relationship between civil and architectural engineers. In producing old Jerusalem, the civil and architectural engineers had been both practical and visionary; maybe they had been one and the same to be able to produce such outstanding work.

After mailing the card, I went to a phone booth to call my parents back at the camp in Lebanon. Since there is no direct phone connection between Israel and Lebanon, I was able to make the call via the Cyprus phone line. Using coded words in case the phones were being bugged by government authorities, I told them about my interview, where I was, and that I would be leaving in two days to return to San Diego.

RAMALLAH AND BEIT LAHAM (BETHLEHEM)

Since I had not had much sleep the night before, I made sure to go to bed early for a good rest on my second night in the holy city. I got up early the next morning and went downstairs for coffee and breakfast. I found out that the waiter came from the city of Ramallah. He shared with me his daily travails waking up very early to get to his job. Ramallah was less than ten miles from the city, yet this poor waiter had to spend about three hours every morning to get between his home and his job. I asked how best to go to Ramallah and Beit Laham. He gave me directions for the minibus pickup point to Ramallah, and from there it would be easy for me to find a ride to Beit Laham.

My trip to Ramallah was relatively uneventful. Arriving in the city, I did not know where to go or what to do. I just started to walk the streets in the small downtown area. Then I remembered from my college days that I had had a neighbor who was studying to be a pharmacist and whose dad owned a pharmacy in Ramallah. As I was wandering around, I walked into a pharmacy to seek my old neighbor. I surmised that the town was small enough that practitioners of the same profession might be quite likely to at least know of each other. The pharmacist indicated that the pharmacy I was seeking was located on the other side of town. I was not sure how far that was and decided I did not have time to seek it out, and so I started to look for the taxi rank for taxis to the city of Beit Laham. Soon I found myself walking into a large open vegetable market. It was late morning and the carts were full of fresh, colorful vegetables and fruits. I pulled out a camera and took several photos of the market, the vegetables and the sellers. I have been told that I have a good eye for pictures, and really believed that one of the colorful market photos I took that day would be worth enlarging. Again, I never got the chance to find out as fate was to change my plans drastically in just a few short hours.

Having stumbled upon the location of the Beit Laham cabs, I hopped into a waiting taxi to visit my second destination of the day. The drive to the city took more than an hour. I found out later that the driver used circuitous routes to avoid Israeli military checkpoints. There *were* short-cuts, but native Palestinians were not allowed to use the special roads which were dedicated exclusively for "illegal" Jewish settlers. We finally arrived at the taxi parking lot just outside the famous Manger Square. I was dismayed as I walked toward the Church of Nativity to see empty Palestinian shops and idle street vendors sitting around the corners, waiting for customers. The Church of Nativity stood tall like a medieval fortress in the center of the city.

Unlike the large entrances you typically see in old buildings, the entry door leading into the church was short. One can still see the original arched gate much higher than the less-than-four-feet-high entryway in use today. The story goes that the entryway was lowered to prevent horses from entering the church. Others maintained it was lowered so that people had to bow as a sign of respect as they entered the church; thus it's name, the "Door of Humility". Inside, the church was rather dark but for the natural light from the high windows. The church's altar was straight ahead. To the right, steps led to the Grotto of the Nativity at the lower level. The supposed exact spot of Jesus' birth was marked with a silver star surrounded by beautiful white marble.

HEAD CONCUSSION AND EMERGENCY ROOM

I finished touring the site in the mid-afternoon and headed back to the taxi rank to catch a ride back to Jerusalem. I remember the car as an old Mercedes with three rows of seating in the back. I sat in the middle row by the window. A young Palestinian college student who sat next to me asked the driver to drop him at his school in a Jerusalem suburb called Abu Deis. I recall the taxi going down the road and turning left where you can see a nice view of the Palestinian villages surrounding the City of Beit Laham. That is about all I remember of my ride back to Jerusalem. I know of the rest from stories I have heard from other people.

Just before we reached Jerusalem, in a town called Al Azzariah, the taxi collided with an Israeli bus. I was knocked unconscious. I do not have any recollection of the accident. Actually, I do not have any memory of anything after seeing the villages on the outskirts of Beit Laham. I was told that

Israeli paramedics had had to use the "Jaws of Life" to get me out of the twisted vehicle. The hospital report indicated that I tried to walk by myself when the ambulance arrived at the emergency room of the Hadassah Hospital. I had a serious head concussion. I suffered lacerations that needed multiple stitches on both sides of my forehead. My chest and left leg were also badly battered. In addition, my vision became unfocused and blurry.

The Hadassah Hospital staff must have found my passport and informed the US embassy, which in turn called my wife in the middle of the night, California time, to tell her that I had been involved in a car accident and had been admitted to the emergency room. When asked about my condition, the embassy personnel told Taghrid that I had suffered a serious head injury and the hospital was going to run another scan to determine if I had a brain hemorrhage. My youngest brother Abdel Nasser was living with us at the time, and was informed of the embassy's phone call. The first thing he did was to try to find someone who could visit me in the hospital. Meanwhile, Taghrid started to make arrangements to travel to Jerusalem. Early in the morning, they contacted my good friend in San Diego, Yousef, who was from a village next to Beit Laham. My brother also contacted a friend of his who came from Jerusalem. My sister asked another friend from the same city for help. Then they called my cousins in Denmark to find out if they had any contact with our relatives who had stayed in the Galilee area following the 1948 *Nakba*. All the contacts were fruitful. By the second day, I had received more visitors in my room than the local patients in the hospital.

The hospital room did not have a phone line. At first, when I received calls, the nurse had to wheel me to the main counter to answer the phone. This trip back and forth to the counter in the main floor lobby became physically overwhelming both for me and the nurses. As a result, callers were told that I was too tired and could not be brought from the room. When my friend Yousef found out, he contacted a buddy of his in Jerusalem and asked him to supply me with a mobile phone. I wasn't aware of what was going on around me, and vaguely remember being wheeled to answer the phone. For that matter, I do not remember talking to people on the phone the first day. Even though my short-term memory was completely lost following the accident, I do remember that at one stage there was a phone next to my bed. I had no idea it was a private phone.

In the hospital, I was under the care of a Palestinian nurse from a town called Beit Sfafa. The nurse must have taken good care of me, for I recall more about her than a lot of other things that happened while in the hospital. I knew of at least one acquaintance many years earlier in California who came from the nurse's village. The small town was well known because, following the 1948 conflict, the demarcation line between Israel and the West Bank divided the village into two parts, each in a different country. Members of the same family were separated and could only meet and communicate by shouting across the barbed wire divide.

The nurse tried to explain to me that I was in Hadassah Hospital, Ein Kerem. Something flashed in my head when I told her that an elementary school in my refugee camp was named after the village of Ein Kerem. My short-term memory must have been making some recovery, because I also have a faint recollection of lying in bed alone, while a young person dressed in a black Orthodox Jewish outfit with long sideburns stood for a long time by the door and gazed straight at me. I stared back hard, and it seemed like a clash of wills, until he left. At the time, I did not know where I was or what was happening around me and was physically powerless, almost paralyzed in bed.

Early in the morning next day, my dad's first cousin, Abu Ali, from the Galilee, received a call from Denmark informing them that the son of their relative Krayem had been admitted to Hadassah Hospital in Ein Kerem. Abu Ali ran to his son-in-law, Abu Ass'ad, catching him before he left for work to share the news. They decided to drive to the hospital along with Abu Ali's wife and her sister, the daughters of Amsha, my father's aunt. Later, Abu Ass'ad told me that after getting my room number from the information counter at the lobby, they walked into a room full of four patients sleeping deeply. They looked at each one trying to guess which one was their blood relative, when they stopped by my bed and decided to take a chance and call out my name. I opened my eyes and fuzzily saw an older person in Arab head garb, a younger man and two older women dressed in traditional Palestinian clothing. I struggled to focus my eyes and looked back and forth trying to figure out if I was in a trance or awake. They stood still, waiting for a response, when I focused on the two ladies for a few seconds and calmly asked if they were Amsha's daughters. They started to weep uncontrollably, hugged and kissed me as if I was their long lost son. I realized then it was not a dream and I became emotional too. I was not sure if I cried because I was happy to see them or because I had been alone and they had jumped at the opportunity to visit me while stricken in hospital. They told me later that my calling their mother's name had been the highlight of our reunion. They had not expected me to know her name, least of all to refer to them as Amsha's daughters twenty years after she had passed away.

Later that same day, Abu Ass'ad went to pick up my wife from Tel Aviv Airport. When she walked into the room, I put my foot in it by introducing the nurse to Taghrid as my other wife at the hospital. I am not sure, I may have been in a fatuous kidding mood or still soporific with the coma medication. Nevertheless, I was certainly and subconsciously touched by the nurse's care. Taghrid took my silly remark in her stride and laughed it away.

I later found out also that my sister had managed to make a three-way phone connection between San Diego, the camp and the hospital. My oldest brother Ghazi inquired whether the accident had taken place before or after I had called them two days earlier. "When did I call you?" I responded. My question terrified the family. They feared the worst about the state of my memory. However, once the doctors were satisfied there was definitely no brain hemorrhage, I was released two or three days later.

Our newfound relatives took us to stay with them at their home in the Palestinian town of Shfa Ammer in the northern Galilee. We stayed in the town for a couple of days while we made new return flight arrangements to San Diego. I still had no short-term memories, but Taghrid later told me that I had acted extremely strangely while staying at their place. She indicated that whenever I left the living room for even a minute, coming back I would reintroduce myself and shake everyone's hand as if I had never met them before. In addition, very often, I would ask her about the people in the room, who they were and what they wanted. For a while also, I lost my sense of taste and could no longer distinguish between different food flavors. I could not sense the flavor of salt, spices, or pickled olives, which I loved. I first thought it was how the food was prepared in my newfound relatives' home and I was uncomfortable bringing up the issue or even asking for salt. Not until I arrived back home in California did I realize that I was missing my tongue's taste receptors as well as my short-term memory.

My original airline ticket had been lost or destroyed in the accident, as had my two cameras. As it is next-to-impossible for one to catch the exact same scenery on two different occasions, I was really saddened by the loss of the recorded pictorial memory of my first trip to my ancestrial home. Our relatives drove us to the TWA offices in Jerusalem a couple of times to get new tickets. I slept most of the time in the car as I was much disoriented, and still have a weak memory of our stay in Shfa Ammer. Taghrid visited the site of her father's destroyed village where her grandparents had lived before they were also expelled to Lebanon in 1948.

We finalized the new flight reservations, and Abu Ass'ad drove us to Tel Aviv Airport on Thanksgiving Day in 1996. I understood from my wife that the Israeli security at a checkpoint outside the airport extensively questioned Abu Ass'ad (putatively an Israeli citizen) before allowing him to proceed to the main building. Inside, once more security was ready to give us the special treatment typically bestowed on anyone visiting Gaza or the West Bank, even more so if they happened also to have Arabic-sounding names and features. The Israeli security moved us to the side for questioning and kept going between us and our relatives, who were waiting in the departure hallway, to compare the answers. Most of what took place at the airport was relayed to me later by Taghrid. At one point, the security asked me about my job. I told them that I worked as an engineer for the City of San Diego. They requested my professional business card. As I handed it to them, I asked, "Why do you need it? Are you planning to call me?" Taghrid mentioned that they did not like my rhetorical question. In addition, my wife started to complain, "Have you no compassion? Can't you see the laceration on his forehead? Let him at least sit down." At that point they decided to bring our checked-in luggage for a second inspection. Departure time was nearing as the security men took their time, unconcerned with my physical condition or the departure schedule. At the last minute, we barely made it to the plane as the door had already been closed and had to be reopened just for us.

Whether one believes in destiny or not, things must happen for a good reason. I was convinced that fate had taken me to Jerusalem to connect me with my long-lost relatives after fifty years of compulsory separation.

Normally, I detest the long transatlantic flights. They are too long and I cannot sleep or relax on the plane. However, that long flight to New York was one of the best transatlantic flights I had flown. Still soporific from my medication, I slept throughout, and when I was awoken, I did not remember much about the flight.

Several months after the accident, I had the chance to go back to the Haddasah Hospital, to visit the relative of a friend of mine. I looked up the nurse to thank her, as a lucid person this time, but was told she was on bereavement leave. I have no memory of what she looked like, or even her name; yet again, she was another person I never got the opportunity to thank for her help during a time of great difficulty in my life.

Note

‒‒

1   Nashashibi, Issam M., 'Remembering Pain Heals Wounds', *The San Diego Union Tribune*, 7 April 2002.

9

The Destruction of Nahr el Bared Camp: The Unrecorded Story

——

Nahr el Bared Camp, the second most populated Palestinian refugee camp in Lebanon, was completely demolished by the Lebanese army in the summer of 2007.

Prior to its destruction, Nahr el Bared was just one of several refugee camps established in Lebanon and elsewhere for Palestinians who had been expelled from their homes in historical Palestine following the creation of the State of Israel in 1948.

There were various stories as to why the camp was established at its eventual location. One story alleged that the Lebanese government wanted to reduce the number of Palestinian refugees by moving them to Syria. After Syria purportedly closed its borders, the trucks had to stop and unloaded the refugees in a large vacant field between the city of Tripoli and the Syrian borders.

However, in talking with many of the camp's elders – who had been actively involved in the selection of the site – I heard a different and more credible story: it was understood that the government wanted to move the Palestinians to the north to reduce the concentration of refugees in southern Lebanon, hence avoiding potential tension with the newly created state of Israel. Refugees were transported on cargo trains toward the penultimate train station in northern Lebanon. Refugees took shelter first in the vacant old French military barracks next to the train depot at the port city of Tripoli. Meanwhile, refugee agencies led by the League of Red Cross Societies (LRCS) and American Friends Service Committee (Quakers) started to look for a piece of land to house these Palestinians. Ein Al Burj farms, some three miles to the south of the current location was the first site to be considered. While the LRCS and Quakers had not been able to secure that deal, they *were* able to lease the current, larger open area, which was partially planted with fava beans. Palestinians from the old French barracks were relocated to this location, while others were taken to another site called Al Khan,* an area closer to the center of the city. The rest of the original camp inhabitants were relocated from A'njar in eastern Lebanon.

Sixty years later, the refugee camp's 40,000‡ inhabitants were again turned into refugees, this time from the camp itself; for many, it was the second or third time in their lives

---

* Al Khan refugees were relocated in the late 1950s to what became Al Badawi Camp, following a major flood in the city.

‡ According to UNRWA records, the registered refugees in the camp numbered circa 27,000. Some of the residents who were registered originally in other camps in Lebanon were not counted as official residents. The majority of the "non-official inhabitants" moved from the south following the Israeli invasion in 1982, and from camps destroyed by Israel invasions or Lebanese Christian right-wing forces during the Lebanese Civil War, e.g. Al Nabatia, Tel Al Zatar, Jisr El Basha, Dikwaneh, etc.

they had been made refugees. The camp was destroyed in the aftermath of a clash between the Lebanese army and Fatah al Islam, a radical local Islamist group that used the camp as a base for their organizational activities.

WHO ARE FATAH AL ISLAM?

There was no universal agreement in the camp, or indeed outside, as to how this organization came into existence. One thing is certainly agreed upon: the group was founded by a charismatic and committed individual named Shaker al Abssi, in association with local Lebanese and other Arab Islamists. Abssi, a Palestinian from Jordan, was a fighter pilot trained by Fatah in the late 1970s before joining a small splinter group known as Fatah al Intifada in the 1980s. Fatah al Intifada broke away from the leading Fatah organization in 1983. The mainstream Fatah group was founded by the late Palestinian president, Yasser Arafat, in 1965. According to people close to the reclusive leader of this organization, Abssi's religious proclivity deepened during three years of incarceration in Syrian jails. Abssi had previously been accused of being an accessory in the killing of an American diplomat in Jordan by a Jordanian court.

Following his release from jail in Syria and his return to Fatah al Intifada, Abssi approached Abu Khalid Al Emleh, the second-highest ranking official in Fatah al Intifada, with a proposal to create a secretive, hence autonomous military branch concentrating its efforts on the Western Division, a code name for military activities inside the occupied Palestinian territories. Emleh and Abssi used their relationship for different purposes. Abssi understood and exploited the internal discord in Fatah al Intifada's leadership to gain access to funding, while Emleh used Abssi to further strengthen his stature inside the organization's leadership structure.

After gaining strength and influence, Abssi took over Fatah al Intifada's centre on the outskirts of Nahr el Bared Camp and declared the creation of a new organization, Fatah al Islam, in November 2006. The group soon became a magnet for local and regional pious Muslims. Sources from inside the camp have indicated that, for the most part, Fatah al Islam was neither a coherently led organization nor an indigenous Palestinian phenomenon. Indeed, 85 per cent of its members were not Palestinians, and its membership included at least forty individuals who claimed they had been involved in fighting against the American occupation forces in Iraq. The organization was a loose coalition of three factions: Abssi represented a relatively moderate faction; Nasser Ismail was a sympathizer with an Islamist group called Jund Al Sham, which had a presence in another Palestinian camp in southern Lebanon; and Abu Huraira was a former Lebanese thug turned Islamist who was associated with the Lebanese Sunni militants pardoned by the Lebanese government in May 2006 as part of a deal to release convicted killer and head of the right-wing "Lebanese Forces" party, Sameer Ja'ja. Personally, I believe that the release of the Sunni militants was part of the Lebanese government's (both Christian and Sunni Muslim) short-sighted policies to offset the "balance of power" and to counter the Shi'a sect's influence manifested by the Hezbollah military group. Huraira represented the extreme wing within the new organization. Ismail, a childhood acquaintance of mine, was the only person in the organizational leadership who was indigenous to the camp.

Like Hamas in the occupied Palestinian territories, Fatah al Islam was inspired by faith and sought to instill Islamic values into the daily life of the Palestinian refugees and in their fighting strategy against Israel. The organization found readily fertile ground in the refugee camp, where for over thirty-seven years the nationalist, internationalist and pan-nationalist organizations had failed to either improve life or achieve the long-held dream of returning the refugees to their original homes. The group's members lived by the virtues they preached. Unlike the other groups in the camp, members of Fatah al Islam treated others with deference.

I had a great many discussions with individuals who disagreed with Fatah al Islam's clash with the Lebanese army, but at the same time, they expressed nothing but praise for members of this organization. People were impressed by their "respectful" demeanor and their apparent genuineness. Fatah al Islam took it upon itself to reach out to rehabilitate those who were perceived as decadent individuals and/or harmful to public security. They tried to rectify and address moral corruption by talking directly to the individual, chivalrously at first, to lead by example and, if all else failed, they were not reluctant to use coercion. I was told how they used to approach teenagers to encourage them to mend their mischievous ways and how some of the teenagers were so impressed they ended up joining the group. In one case, they failed to stop an alcoholic person from drinking and cursing God in public; but he learned how to behave in their presence.

Simply put, the camp inhabitants, similar to the people of Gaza and the West Bank when they voted for Hamas, were yearning for a moral authority. The people in the camp were fed up with the empty promises of the traditional leading organizations and their evident political impotency and moral corruption.

THE CREATION OF FATAH AL ISLAM
Following the destruction of the camp, questions were raised as to how this organization had come into existence and

whether there had been official Lebanese government collusion in the growth of the new Sunni organization, especially since some members of the group had been able to travel overtly from their traditional base in southern Lebanon to the north. Huraira's faction transported Arab volunteers openly from both Beirut's airport and the Syrian border, passing through several Lebanese military checkpoints. Individuals I talked to had very good reasons to believe that at first Fatah al Islam was encouraged or sanctioned by the government. The government turned a blind eye to the growing military capabilities of this Sunni group by allowing them to transfer weapons through army checkpoints surrounding the camp. Like the American government's past support for the Taliban Mujahedeen in their fight against the Soviet Union in Afghanistan in the 1980s, and the Israeli policies that prompted the rise of Hamas to counter the legitimacy of the PLO, the Lebanese government failed to understand the strategic flaws in its myopic political agenda for a factional "balance of power". Lebanese leaders, mainly the prime minister's party prior to May 2007, hoped that the new militaristic Sunni organization would counterbalance the power of the Shia Hezbollah.

This allegation is further supported by formal money transactions delivered from sources in Saudi Arabia via the Mediterranean Bank of Lebanon. Members of this group received regular monthly transfers from the bank's branch at Al Kalamoon, a small town located several miles south of the city of Tripoli. However, when in May 2007, Fatah al Islam members went to pick up their monthly money transfer, the bank refused to release the funds. Next day, members of this group took over the bank and forced the release of their seized money. It was stated that the group confiscated only the amount held in their name with the bank. Lebanese

Internal Security traced the perpetrators to a Fatah al Islam safe house in the city of Tripoli. The Lebanese Internal Security carried out a well publicized raid on their hiding place in the city and several people on both sides were killed or injured. It is worth noting here that the Internal Security foray was not coordinated with the Lebanese army. Immediately following the raid, news reached Fatah al Islam in Nahr el Bared Camp that their comrades were being "massacred" at the hands of the Lebanese security forces. In retribution, Huraira led a surprise attack against a Lebanese army post outside the camp. The army contingent had no knowledge of the conflict in Tripoli; Huraira's group murdered several of the unsuspecting officers to avenge the killing of their members earlier that morning.

The reckless action by members of Fatah al Islam against the Lebanese army post was condemned fervidly by camp residents as well as the various Palestinian political organizations. Large public demonstrations blocked the main road to protest Fatah al Islam's irresponsible attempts to drag the camp into a confrontation with the Lebanese army. Nevertheless, immediately following the murder of their soldiers, the Lebanese army set a tight siege around the camp and threatened to attack unless Fatah al Islam members surrendered themselves to the army. In less than twenty-four hours, the Lebanese army cordoned all access and started to bomb the camp indiscriminately. The army fusillade was not limited to known positions of Fatah al Islam on the outskirts of the camp. It targeted the main souk and the most densely populated areas inside the camp proper.

As a sign of support for the Lebanese army, all major Palestinian political and military organizations ordered their members and supporters to evacuate the camp at once. During the first two weeks of the indiscriminate shelling, about 30,000 people fled the camp. My elderly parents, along with about 10,000 other residents, refused to leave. Power and water were cut off immediately following the blockade on 20 May 2007. At the time, my parents' mobile phone, their only contact with the outside world, was kept charged by a car battery. Our frequent phone calls were regularly interrupted by the shrill sounds of explosions and people howling for help. During one of our phone conversations, my mother remarked that the mass flight from the camp brought back the sixty-year-old dreadful memories of their forced departure from their homes in Palestine. Like those who remained, my parents were determined not to become refugees again.

Until the first week of June 2007, international aid convoys were still able to bring in badly needed supplies to the remaining population during lulls in the gunfire. The Lebanese army, however, was getting frustrated with the delivery of aid, and wanted all civilians to evacuate the camp. Consequently, the army attacked an approaching UN convoy in broad daylight. The Lebanese army at first claimed that Fatah al Islam was responsible for shooting at the UN vehicles. However, I talked to two of the drivers in the aid convoy who maintained that the shooting clearly came from Lebanese army positions. One of the drivers, my younger brother, was saved only by the grace of God in the shelling. The UN vehicle he was driving received a direct hit and was separated from the main group. For long agonizing hours, he was lost and feared dead. As a result, the UN was forced to cease its humanitarian aid activities and started to arrange for the "forced" evacuation of the remaining civilians. My parents were part of the last medical convoy departing Nahr el Bared on 10 June 2007.

My mother's dreadful apprehension was realized again almost sixty years after her first expulsion from her native home in Palestine. She, my father, and over 40,000 of the camp's residents became refugees again. Just like during their first flight in 1948, they had no choice but to start their lives from scratch all over again: tragically, all their sixty years of accrued memories and possessions were lost during the obliteration.

THE DESTRUCTION OF THE CAMP

The camp had a very high population density, with over 40,000 inhabitants living in an area less than one square mile. Fatah al Islam numbered less than 200 fighters (a spokesman of the organization claimed in the Lebanese press that the number was 98 fighters). Their defending positions were located on the north side, in an area known as the new camp, near the SAMED building.* However, from day one of the fighting, the Lebanese army bombarded the camp indiscriminately and did not limit the shelling to Fatah al Islam fighting positions. The Lebanese government, abetted by the conspicuous silence of the Palestinian leadership, ordered the camp inhabitants to evacuate their homes in preparation for their final assault. Camp inhabitants were promised compensation and were assured that their homes would be rebuilt as soon as the army rid the camp of this organization. A large number of camp residents trusted their leadership and the assurances of the Lebanese government and left their homes.

---

* The SAMED building was a well-known landmark building on the outskirts of the camp. SAMED is an Arabic acronym for Palestine Martyrs Works Society. It was initially created by the PLO in 1970 to provide vocational training to martyrs' children and widows. In later years, SAMED became the PLO business institution dealing in trade, investment, etc. This particular building also served as a garment factory which also provided training for women in the camp.

At the start of the fighting, the Lebanese military put Fatah al Islam fighters at 300. Even if one were to accept this official estimate, Fatah al Islam would not have been able to have more than 80 per cent of its fighting force at the front at any one time. Their total fighting power could not have exceeded 250 able fighters. Thus, it would have been impossible for the less than 300 fighters to have maintained a physical presence in all areas of the camp, comprising more than 6,000 homes.

This supports the theory held by many in the camp that the destruction of Nahr el Bared was an end in itself and Fatah al Islam was merely a pretext to remove yet another Palestinian camp from the Lebanese landscape.

I talked with the very few people who remained in the camp beyond 10 June 2007. All corroborated the assertion that, from the outset, the military concentrated its shelling on the residential areas and not on Fatah al Islam's defending positions. In this case, the Lebanese army followed the same tactics employed by the Israeli military strategists of overwhelming and indiscriminate military bombardment, especially on civilian targets, to create a rift between the fighters and the surrounding population. Most of the Lebanese soldiers lost in the battle were killed in counterattacks carried out by Fatah al Islam on military positions, and very few of the soldiers were killed in fighting inside the camp. Killing or apprehending members of Fatah al Islam could have been done without obliterating the entire residential community. The less than 300 fighters (accepting the army official estimate) could have been surrounded and the battle could have been limited to a small section of the camp. Being a person who is admittedly naïve in military tactics, I would suspect that limiting the fight to a small open area would have been easier than negotiating the myriad circuitous alleys in the old camp;

unless, of course, the intention was to destroy the camp and not Fatah al Islam.

It took the Lebanese national army more than four months of nonstop blitzkrieg to destroy and seize control of the camp from a comparably small number of fighters. After their entry, the army completed its job through systematic looting and an operation to destroy the remaining standing shelters. I talked to individuals who were able to get into their homes in the area known as the "new camp" in October 2007, soon after it fell into the Lebanese army's hands. These individuals indicated that, for the most part, they found their homes in acceptable condition, but when they returned days later, they discovered their homes had been either destroyed or burned down. One person in the "new camp" said that the army had attempted to blow up his house long after seizing the area. Apart from some broken windows and busted walls, the house had been in good structural condition. But when the owner returned to the house several days later, he found out that explosions had been set off next to the concrete columns (I observed this damage and offered professional recommendations for proper structural column restoration). However, because of army incompetence, while the explosions had exposed the steel rebar, it had failed to demolish the house as the roof load was transferred to the remaining standing walls. I have several photos of racist graffiti written inside the home. To cover up the looting, the army drenched the walls with flammable liquid and attempted to burn down the house. The orderly looting in fact was observed as late as December 2008, while the army continued to recover and ship out troves uncovered during the formal military clean-up and debris removal from the old camp.

Palestinian women, young and old, pride themselves on the gold or jewelry in their possession. Most married women in the camp invest their dowry money in buying gold as a safety net for a rainy day. Countless stories were shared about women who were not able to find their gold savings when they were granted a fifteen-minute inspection of the homes several months later. Their houses had been looted, burned or imploded during the period following the formal military operation.

I talked to one individual who was lamenting the loss of his wife's gold, worth over $5,000, and that of his mother-in-law's jewelry which had been entrusted to him for safe keeping. Since a good number of people had little faith in the banking system, their hidden cash savings at home had vanished too. When I asked one person why he didn't collect his valuables during the evacuation, he said, "The bombardment was indiscriminate, and saving the family and children was my first priority; after all, we all assumed it was going to be a brief skirmish and we would be back in our homes in a day or two at the most. We never expected to come back to flattened homes."

In a letter to the Lebanese prime minister dated 31 October 2007 (MDE 18/015/2007), Amnesty International expressed its concerns regarding the reported looting and abuse by the army. The letter stated in part:

> Many homes were reported to have been looted of their most valuable possessions, such as televisions, fridges, washing-machines, jewelry and money, some shops have also been looted and one community center has had its electricity generator taken. A number of homes also appear to have been deliberately set on fire since the fighting ended, evidenced by remains of car-tires, gas canisters used to start fires and stains from inflammable liquid sprayed onto walls ... At least three houses are reported to have been badly damaged or destroyed without justification in the weeks after the end of fighting.

Another person, who was more fortunate, confided to me that his mother's jewelry was delivered to her several months after she had left the camp. The gold was recovered by an individual they never met or knew. The story goes that during the heavy fighting, a group of women who were married to members of Fatah al Islam took shelter with their children in his mother's home in July 2007. During their stay, one woman who was pregnant went into labor. The women in the group took the liberty of helping themselves to towels and sheets from the closet, when they came across the gold jewelry hidden in the cupboard. A woman in the group recognized a picture on the wall of a child attending the same preschool as her toddler and decided to take the jewelry with her as they were getting ready to evacuate the camp. The women and children of Fatah al Islam members were granted safe passage in late August 2007. After settling in one of the Palestinian camps in south Lebanon, the woman gave the name of the child (whose picture was on the wall) to a confidant and asked him to look the child up in one of the refugee shelters in north Lebanon. After locating the child, the woman entrusted an individual to deliver the jewelry to the child's mother. Believing her gold had been lost forever, the woman couldn't believe the return of her life savings.

CLOSED MILITARY AREA

The army did not allow any access to the "old camp" for several months after seizing control of the area in September 2007. They initially claimed that many of the homes had been booby-trapped by Fatah al Islam. This was repudiated by homeowners who alleged that for the most part more than 65 per cent of the homes were salvageable; if not structurally at least a great part of their possessions could have been retrieved and saved. According to homeowners who eventually were able to enter the camp, there were two kinds of destruction: some homes had been severely damaged by the shelling, but others had been flattened by implosions after the army entered the camp. The methodical structural destruction and looting gave birth to a new Arabic rhyme to describe the army's actions, which when translated into English reads, "the army was fighting bricks [*hajar*] and not humans [bachar]".

This was especially true since many members of the Fatah al Islam leadership were able to flee the camp during and after the battle, despite the supposedly watertight military siege. In fact, Huraira, the Lebanese military head of the organization, was killed several days after the end of military operations in a clash with police positions in the city of Tripoli some ten miles south of the camp. The apparent second-in-command, Nasser Ismail, was arrested weeks later, some eight miles further south in another Palestinian camp, Badawi. Nasser was turned over by Palestinian security forces to the Lebanese army. The head of Fatah al Islam, Abssi, was also believed to have survived the army onslaught. According to sources, he hid near the city of Tripoli for a short period before being smuggled out of Lebanon inside boxes on the back of a vegetable truck. He has now disappeared, most likely having been arrested or killed in Syria.

Immediately after the conclusion of military operations, camp residents were anxious to go back and check on their homes. Up until then, they had taken refuge at UN schools, in vacant structures in the Badawi camp or garage buildings and improvised shelters in the vicinity. People who were made refugees for the second or third times in their lifetimes were hoping to be able to go back soon to inspect the remnants of their homes. But, contrary to the continued promises from the Lebanese prime minister, the army refused to allow inhabitants access to their homes. To further delay the return of refugees, the prime minister spoke of the need to settle land ownership claims before permitting the return of refugees or the commencement of construction work. The homecoming became a contentious issue between UNRWA, the UN agency in charge of the welfare of Palestinian refugees, and the Lebanese government. The UNRWA field director was accredited for the most part in swaying the international community to pressure the Lebanese government to stick to its obligations toward Palestinian refugees. At the same time as the UNRWA field director was receiving high praise for his tireless efforts on behalf of the camp's refugees, the Palestinian Authority representative in Lebanon, Abbas Zaki, was being ridiculed for his conspicuous incompetence in resolving the conflict at the outset of the fighting and his failure to ease the people's hardship following the destruction of the camp.

Responding to pressure from regional and international human rights organizations on the Lebanese government, months later, the army started to issue special military permits to camp inhabitants, granting them permission to inspect the remains of their homes. Starting in January 2008, a handful of new permits were issued to residents each day. Like everything else in Lebanon, individuals with good connections were given preference and received permits first. Residents were thoroughly searched before being allowed to inspect their properties. Cameras or cell phones with cameras were not allowed in, and people were searched again on their way back from the camp for valuables. Each permitted party was provided with fifteen minutes to collect small salvageable items and was assigned a soldier to watch them carefully while inspecting the ruins, making sure no pictures were taken.

The camp's narrow alleys were completely blocked by rubble. Residents had to walk over the devastated houses to reach the area where their homes once stood. On the way to inspect their ruins, homeowners were exposed to insulting and racist graffiti on what remained of the standing structures. One common graffiti phrase was "*Shater, Shater elie Be'rif Beitu*" (or "Smart, smart, he who can identify their home"). Family pictures and religious frames had been maliciously smashed and covered with human excrement. I spoke with many people who had been allowed to inspect their destroyed homes and almost all talked about their ignominious and horrid treatment at the hand of army officers before and after being allowed to accompany a Lebanese soldier to conduct the fifteen-minute inspection visit. Despite this, some also talked about the benevolent behavior of a few of the military escorts as they grieved the ruins of their homes.

Following the land deed issue, the Lebanese government claimed that they still had not secured the international aid for the rebuilding. When the donor money became available, and to gain political favor in the parliamentary elections in summer 2009, the Lebanese faction controlling the government distributed a sizable portion of the aid earmarked for the camp's rebuilding efforts to voters in neighboring Lebanese villages who were purportedly "impacted economically" by the fighting. By January 2010, most of the extensively damaged multi-story buildings in the new camp (the area abutting the old camp) remained a closed military area and were not turned over to their registered owners. A small part of the severely damaged sector had been handed over several months earlier, but unlike the "economically" impacted bordering villages, the owners of these destroyed structures were told that no donor money was available to help rebuild their shattered homes.

In summer 2009, a right-wing Lebanese group filed a court injunction to prevent pre-construction activities under the pretext of uncovering historical artifacts beneath the rubble of the destroyed homes. This was an area that had been disturbed by construction for over sixty years and where every single home had an underground septic tank. It turned out that the specious artifacts were nothing more than the "serendipitous discovery" of large, natural stones that had originally been used in the destroyed homes, underground walls for the septic tanks, or clay pipes serving these underground structures.

At the time of writing in March 2010, entry to the old camp is not allowed and access to the new camp is controlled by strict security measures where cars are thoroughly searched and only holders of special permits are allowed in and out of the new camp area.

REASONS FOR THE DESTRUCTION OF THE CAMP

As expounded above, the clash between the Lebanese army and Fatah al Islam could have been limited to a small area or a section of the camp. However, it was evident from the start that the army stratagem had been to bomb population centers in order to pressure people to flee their homes. On the surface, no Lebanese official supported the destruction of the camp. All the same, there were always those who covertly had advocated the removal of Palestinian camps in Lebanon for the last forty years. Hence the destruction and then the slaughter of the remaining unarmed population in Tel Al Zatar and two small unofficial camps in east Beirut at the hands of the right-wing Christian militia in 1976; the destruction of Al Nabatia Camp at the hands of Israel in the 1970s and the massacres in Sabra and Shatilla by Lebanese Christian militia with guidance from the Israeli occupying forces in September 1982.

Below is a short analysis of some of the key issues that may have contributed to creating the social and political conditions that led to the demise of the camp:

1   The Middle East Peace Process: The presence of refugee camps was a continued reminder and a manifestation of the 1948 Palestinian tragedy. Israel, the United States and most Arab governments would like to see the refugee camps disbanded for the eventual resettlement of refugees outside Palestine or Israel. The presence of Palestinian refugees in Lebanon, where they are not allowed to work in over seventy skilled trades, has been seen as a serious obstacle to progress in the peace talks between Israel and the Palestinian Authority. Palestinian refugees insist on their right of return to their original homes under UN Resolution 194. Israel, supported by the United States, has vehemently opposed the return of refugees as a threat to the make-up and identity of Israel as an "exclusively" Jewish state.

The Arab governments, while overtly supporting the right of return for refugees, have long oppressed and imposed severe economic and travel restrictions on the movement of Palestinian refugees across their borders, and have ceased calling for the right of return. Instead they now appeal for a "just solution" for Palestinian refugees. Hence, the disappearance of another Palestinian camp is one less political hurdle in the complicated peace process.

It is possible that Israel may even have played an indirect role in the military operation, via its labyrinth of spies in the Lebanese army. In summer 2009, the Lebanese government uncovered a large network of Israeli agents, mainly in active and retired military capacities. Among those arrested was Mansoor Diab, an army major who, according to the Lebanese press, had played a significant role in the destruction of the camp. Diab confessed to having worked for the Israeli intelligence services since the mid-1990s. This was in addition to discovering mysterious engraved Hebrew lettering on large exploded artillery casing found among the rubble during the early inspection visits of the destroyed homes.

2   Lebanese Sectarianism: Palestinian camps in Lebanon represented a threat to "sectarian stability" by upsetting the balance of power between the various religious communities in the country. Lebanon's confessional democracy is held together by a thin thread balancing arrangements across the sectarian divide. The continued presence of mostly Muslim Palestinians (95 per cent of the Christian Palestinians were naturalized in Lebanon in the 1950s and 60s) was seen as a threat to the demographic make-up of the state.

3   Economics: The camp was not directly impacted by the Lebanese Civil War and the many Israeli incursions into Lebanon. The camp's proximity to Syria and its direct access to the sea helped create a relatively strong and vibrant economy, bearing in mind that a substantial percentage of trade in Lebanon is smuggled via the sea or through Lebanon's porous borders with Syria. The camp, like many other communities near the Syrian border or along the shoreline, became a good intermediate station for Lebanese and Syrian illegal traders to smuggle, store and distribute contraband goods throughout Lebanon and Syria.

Despite this, residents in the camp benefited very little economically from the smuggled traffic, as most of the contraband activities were carried out predominantly by large Lebanese traders who only wished to take advantage of the camp's location. Matters became even more complicated since the majority of the Lebanese illegal traders dealing in the camp were associated with the Christian city of Zgharta, the main Lebanese counterpart for the large illegal Syrian traders. The Zgharta traders supported the Lebanese opposition in Lebanon, while the traders in the city of Tripoli and the area surrounding the camp supported the Sunni prime minister's faction.

As explained earlier in the book, the camp became a major trading center in northern Lebanon, competing successfully with similar businesses in the city of Tripoli and surrounding communities. Legitimate local traders in the camp, such as gold merchants, became a serious trading challenge to gold shops in Tripoli. Pharmacies in the camp sold medication at lower prices than Lebanese pharmacies, Medical doctors treated patients at a more reasonable cost. The camp traders had a competitive advantage over Lebanese traders in every aspect since businesses inside the camp enjoyed lower labor costs and benefited from the lack of tax collection in the camp. The value added tax, which was introduced several years ago but was still haphazardly enforced throughout Lebanon, wasn't enforced inside the camp.

Appreciating the economic factor is essential for understanding the motives behind the Lebanese government's resolve to seize and destroy the camp. In layman's terms, the competition created resentment among the Sunni Lebanese merchants who were losing business to the camp. In social and political vernacular, capitalist greed turned competition into latent human resentment. Sunni capitalists' interests were aligned with right-wing Christian–Muslim sectarian politics, in a bid to destroy the camp as part of the indirect fray between the government and the opposition. Arab governments and the international community, and even the Palestinian Authority, provided a cover for the destruction of thousands of homes under the pretext of fighting "Muslim fundamentalists".

THE STRUGGLE TO SURVIVE

The thought of becoming refugees once again was loathed by camp residents. Many had been made homeless again during the Lebanese Civil War and the several Israeli incursions into southern Lebanon. Since 20 May 2007, numerous people who seemed otherwise healthy have suffered serious stress-related health problems. The predominant epidemic was heart attacks and strokes, including my mother and cousin. As a result, more people have passed away since summer 2007 than in any other parallel period since the establishment of the camp in 1949.

Yet many have continued to endure. Part of the time I spent with the camp's residents was just to observe their behavior. To my surprise, they were able to laugh and even make jokes about their predicament. I noticed that when residents first met, the primary question they exchanged was: "Where do you live now?" Many had not met for several months or since May 2007. The follow-up question would be about their possessions and whether they had been able to visit their homes and what they had been able to recover. Most did not recover much.

One woman boasted about recovering three natural gas cylinders. Gas cylinders were expensive and it was typical for homes to have several back-up cylinders at any one time. She recounted the story of finding three salvageable gas cylinders from her property. She decided to retrieve the cylinders following her fifteen-minute supervised inspection. The army officer asked her, "How do you plan to carry the cylinders to the main road?"

She riposted, "You are going to carry two of them for me; isn't it enough you destroyed my home? I should be able to get something back from the army."

The officer replied, "No, I can't."

She responded, "Well, I will sit here until you carry these cylinders or you go and leave me alone, this is my home!"

The army officer relented and ended up helping carry the gas cylinders to the road.

Another story I heard involved an old schoolmate named Faleh. He was sitting on the rubble of his demolished four-story building erected just outside the camp. A friend asked him, "How are you doing?"

Faleh responded with his trademark wit, "I want to thank the Lebanese army for doing me a big favor."

"How was that?"

"Well, before this building was destroyed, I got exhausted daily trying to climb the stairs to reach the top floor. As you can see now, thanks to the efficient work of the Lebanese army, it now takes no effort to reach the top of my building."

Faleh was one of the major tobacco traders in the camp.

Another shared comical story was about the goats that had frightened the Lebanese army. Abu Na'eem was an old man who owned several valuable milking goats of the Shami variety. These are red in color and are known for their valuable prolific milk production. During the heavy bombardment, when Abu Na'eem was grudgingly evacuated from his home, he made sure to leave the barn gate open for the goats. Near his house, there was a farm and natural running water. He wanted to make sure the goats were able to move in and out of the barn to the nearby field for feeding and water. According to some witnesses, the goats used to leave the home in the morning to graze and came back to the barn at dusk. As the fighting got closer and the barn was damaged, the goats took shelter in the thicket fence of bamboo canes around the farm. After the army seized the area, the Lebanese soldiers took positions in the vicinity of the field. At night, the goats attempted to leave their hiding place in the bamboo hedge. As they moved the canes started to flutter, the army was alarmed by the movement and started to shoot toward the shrubbery. In turn, the goats were petrified and started to hop around vigorously, which in turn swayed the canes more intensely. The army continued to shoot and retreated from their positions, fearing an attack by Fatah al Islam or possible ghosts on the farm. Next morning the army discovered the culprits, as several of the goats lay dead. People jokingly called this incident: the night when Abu Na'eem's goats routed the Lebanese army.

Camp residents cherished sharing such funny stories dragged out of a bottomless well of despair. Laughing at their misery must have served as a subconscious therapeutic remedy to alleviate the torment and offered them a temporary break from the melancholy of life.

LOST MEMORY

I tried to understand what it meant for people to lose homes, possessions and their life savings. The experience to most was ineffable. Yet most were less concerned with the physical loss than the loss of their stored historical memories, such as photos of bereaved family members or the memory of the place. Residents were mostly disconcerted they had not been able to recover photos, or had discovered an old framed picture swathed with human faeces. Months following their evacuation, camp residents had given up any hope of seeing their homes again or even recovering their belongings, but they still had some hope that they would be able to recover some of the memories left behind.

I was told the story of an old man who was sitting with a cane on the side of the road while many individuals were lined up at an army checkpoint for permission to visit the rubble of their homes. After checking all the military permits for people in the queue, an army officer noticed the despondent old man still sitting impassively on the side of the road. The officer approached the old man and asked if he could be of any help.

The old man responded, "I just want to visit my home."

The officer asked about the permit, but the old man did not have one.

The wizened man then pleaded with the officer, "If you allow me to enter, I do not plan to bring anything from the house. I just want to look at it; I want to stand in the alley. I want to go and sit on the rubble until I die."

At first, I wasn't able to fully appreciate how painful it could be for one to lose the historical memory of the place. That changed on 8 December 2008. After the loss of their home, my father and bed-stricken mother were staying with my older brother, Majed, who had invested all his money several years earlier on a new plot to build a home on the outskirts of the camp, in what came to be known as the new camp. The house was severely damaged, looted, almost demolished and burned down. Soon after Majed was permitted to move back in, he brought the structure back to minimal livable conditions to shelter his family and homeless elderly parents.

During my visit to the camp in December 2008, residents were planning a ceremony at the camp's old cemetery on the first day of Eid Al Adha. This is the day when Muslims commemorate Patriarch Abraham's willingness to sacrifice his son for God. It is traditional on this day for people to clean and visit the graves of their dead family members. The old cemetery was located in the original camp, a closed military area. On the morning of 8 December, approximately 3,000 residents started to gather at a military post on the northern side of the camp. I joined the gathering as we started to march toward the military rampart. After tense moments, the military relented and opened the road. We all rushed through a massive military dirt fortification. The distance from one end of the camp to the other was little more than half a mile. The road was located on the seaside, which runs by my old neighborhood. It was my first close-up visit to see the devastation left behind. My younger brother Kamal, who had seen the destruction earlier, started to point out some of the supposed familiar places. He pointed to an area full of rubble and said this was our school; this was the house of the old school's janitor; this was the ration center, etc.

I did not recognize any of the scenes that passed before my eyes. The place looked more like a Hollywood film set than a community that had housed more than 40,000 people. And then we reached our neighborhood, and he said this was our play area, and over there you can see the vestige of our childhood home. My brother Majed caught up with us and disagreed about which demolished structure was our home. I was completely befuddled by the tableau. This was the house I had lived in for the first eighteen years of my life, this was the neighborhood where I swam, fished, labored, sold aggregate and bones. This was supposed to be the place of my childhood and adolescent memories. This was the house and the neighborhood I had last visited three years earlier. And yet it bore absolutely no resemblance to anything I could remember.

Although, in my memories, I can still internally visualize my childhood home and neighborhood, the sight of the ruins in front of me felt as if the first eighteen years of my life had been eradicated. The encounter with the destruction allowed me to better understand what Palestinian refugees have gone through during the last sixty years. Despite the new cataclysm, the resolute camp residents, like the phoenix rising from the ashes, established unofficial popular rebuilding committees and composed a new inspiring contemporary slogan: "We will rebuild Nahr el Bared and we shall return to Palestine."

Although it was that much harder to comprehend the loss, I was finally able to fathom the secret of the older generation's eternal connection to Palestine, a nation that continued to exist only in their historical memories. At last, I realized that while for most people shelter and survival are the very highest priorities, this is not so in the hierarchy of the Palestinian refugees. Despite sixty years of *Nakba*, they have remained part of an enduring nation in exile. The dispossession and the challenge to survive have become their very identity and a key component of what it means to be a Palestinian.